The BOX MAKER'S GUITAR *Book*

Sweet-Sounding Design & Build
Projects for Makers & Musicians

The BOX MAKER'S GUITAR Book

Sweet-Sounding Design & Build Projects for Makers & Musicians

DOUG STOWE

SPRING HOUSE PRESS

Publisher: Paul McGahren
Editorial Director: Matthew Teague
Editor: Kerri Grzybicki
Design: Lindsay Hess
Layout: Michael Douglas
Illustration: Carolyn Mosher
Step-by-Step Photography: Doug Stowe
Project and Detail Photography: Danielle Atkins
Maker Gallery Photography: As labeled

Spring House Press
P.O. Box 239
Whites Creek, TN 37189

ISBN: 978-1-940611-64-8

Library of Congress Control Number: 2017952114
Printed in the United States of America
First Printing: August 2017

Many thanks to the maker gallery contributors: Richard Briggs, Ted Crocker,
Kevin Hamilton, Zeke Leonard, Ron Lutz, John McNair, Shane Speal, and
Ed Stilley (Kelly Mulhollan).

Note: The following list contains names used in *The Box Maker's Guitar Book* that
may be registered with the United States Copyright Office: Camacho Liberty; C.B.
Gitty; Clear Spring School; Corian; Dan Sleep-Humidor Guitars; Danny Glover;
Gary Clark, Jr.; Gisbert; *Guitar World;* Humbucker Phat Screamer; Indian Tabac;
Jackson Pollock; Jon Miller; Kahler; Keith Urban; Krusty; *Kubo and the Two Strings;*
Liga Privada Flying Pig; *Los Angeles Times;* Montecristo; NPR; Padron; PBS; Pete
Seeger; *Premier Guitar Magazine;* Punch; Rocky Patel Battalion; *Songs Inside the
Box;* Starr Hill; Stella; *Strung Together;* Swisher Sweets; *The Simpsons; True Faith,
True Light, the Devotional Art of Ed Stilley;* Vaughn; Vermont Natural Coatings.

To learn more about Spring House Press books, or to find a retailer near you,
email info@springhousepress.com or visit us at www.springhousepress.com.

CONTENTS

USING THIS BOOK

Cigar box guitars have become immensely popular, in part because they are relatively easy to make, unlike more conventional guitars. It is also fun to play an instrument that you've had a hand in making. This book takes the trend another step by matching up box making techniques with the popular hobby of making cigar box guitars. By creating your own box, you'll open up a world of customization and finishing options to make a truly unique box guitar. A woodworker with some basic experience and common tools can build their own guitar, from scratch, without professional luthier training.

After beginning with a walk-through of a basic purchased guitar kit in chapter 1 (page 11), the book is organized into chapters that focus on the components of a box guitar. You can mix and match your favorite parts and techniques to create a guitar that's really your own. A gallery of different options appears at the end of each chapter to help you in your selection. Wrapping up the book is an extensive chapter on building a ukulele (page 113), as well as a gallery of photographs from the world of box guitar making (page 145).

Chapter 1: **Making a Kit Guitar**

Use an approachable purchased kit to create your own guitar. This overview will help you make more sense of the following chapters.

Chapter 3: **Necks**

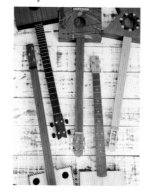

The neck attaches to the body of the guitar on one end, and houses the tuners at the other.

Chapter 2: **Box Sides**

The first part when building your own guitar is the box sides. Guitars have either a sounding box or a solid body in the shape of a sounding box (where one would add electronic components and pickups). The box provides resonance by absorbing the vibration of the strings and communicating that vibration into the air. Crafting the sides of the box body is the first step in creating a guitar.

Chapter 4: **Frets**

Frets are installed either directly into the neck or on a fretboard that is then glued to the neck.

Chapter 5: **Tops and Backs**

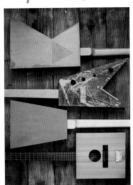

The box is completed with a top and back. Whether you choose book-matched hardwoods or plain lywood, the guitar box will now be completed.

Chapter 6: **Finishing**

Finishing is the next step. Painting, clear finishes, and more are explored here.

Chapter 7: **Tuners and Tailpieces**

Tuners and tailpieces are the two anchor points for the strings. The tuners are at the top of the neck, and the tailpiece is at the bottom of the guitar.

Chapter 8: **Bridges and Nuts**

The bridge communicates the vibration of the strings into the body of the box. Its placement in relation to the nut establishes the required length of the strings to correspond with the placement of the frets. Both parts have notches to hold the strings apart in the right position, and at just the right elevation above the frets.

Chapter 9: **Electrifying Your Guitar**

Electrifying your guitar opens up the world of amps and computers to your music.

Chapter 10: **Making a Uke**

Now that you have a thorough understanding of how to create a guitar, try this tropical variation.

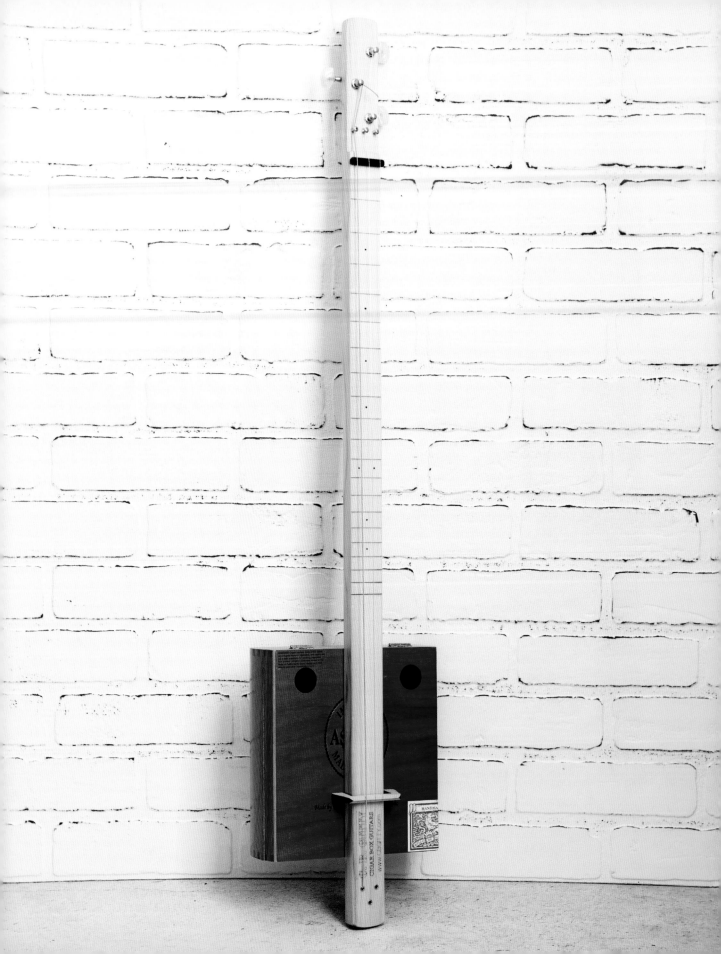

Chapter 1

MAKE *a* KIT GUITAR

Building a kit box guitar is a great way to get familiar with the concepts involved in guitar construction, and the kit built in the following pages was prepared by C.B. Gitty, one of the suppliers of parts for making box guitars and other kinds of stringed instruments. Right out of the box, everything is supplied to get you playing an instrument of your own in minutes. Instead of frets at precise intervals that provide clear places for the fingers to form chords, the neck of the kit guitar has laser-engraved lines that give only a hint of where the fingers might be placed. The lack of real frets, however, gives an amateur musician the opportunity to play the guitar in a different manner, using a finger slide to create the sounds of the blues unrestrained by precise finger placement. With the C.B. Gitty kit, this slide is provided.

Making a kit guitar or watching one be made will get your creative juices flowing and provide a basic understanding of the necessary parts of a box guitar. Let's get started!

TOOLS & MATERIALS

Cigar box guitar kit (we used C.B. Gitty kit #36-005-01A)	Paintbrush	Woodburner
	Sandpaper	Hammer
Danish oil finish (optional)	Pencil	Dowel
	Steel rule	Screwdriver
Water-based urethane finish	Awl	

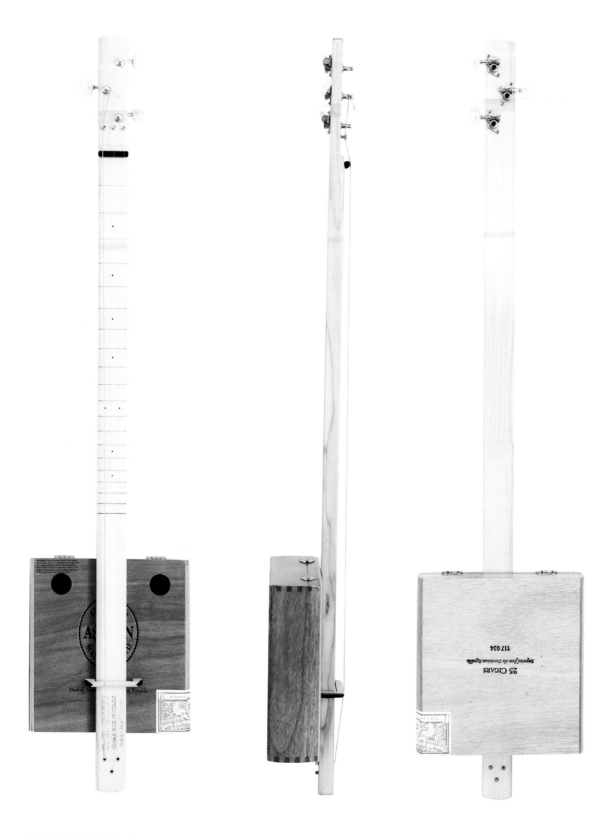

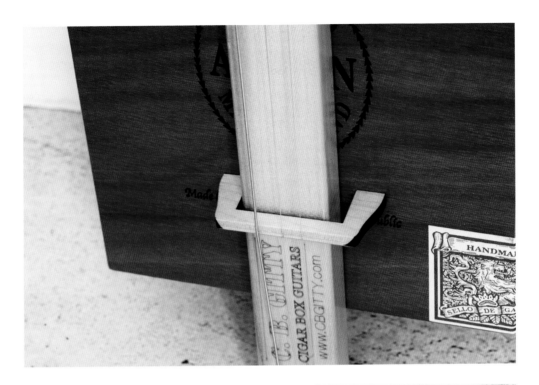

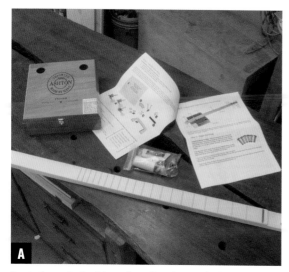

A

Look through the kit and get familiar with the contents.

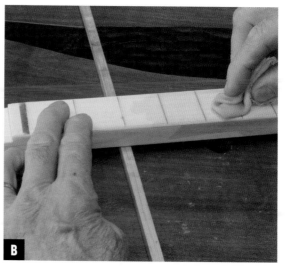

B

Darken the wood by applying Danish oil finish.

GET STARTED

Straight out of the box, the kit contains everything you need, including instructions; unpack everything **(A)**.

You may want to apply Danish oil finish to darken the wood and prepare it for finish **(B)**.

Use water-based urethane finish to protect the neck from wear **(C)**. This will keep it looking nice after hours and hours of play.

C

Brush on a few coats of water-based urethane finish.

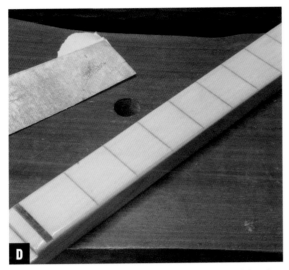

Be sure to sand the neck between applications of finish.

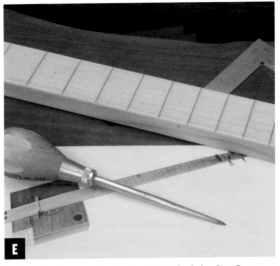

Follow the instructions in the kit to find the fret finger positions and mark them.

Sand lightly between coats of urethane to get the smoothest finish **(D)**.

Locate the fret finger positions **(E)**. Most fretted instruments have markings to indicate the finger positions for the 3rd, 5th, 7th, 9th, 12th, 15th, and 17th frets. The neck that comes in the kit is not marked, but the instructions suggest that you do so. You'll need a pencil, steel rule, and awl to mark as shown in the instructions. Use a woodburner to mark the fret finger position spots **(F)**.

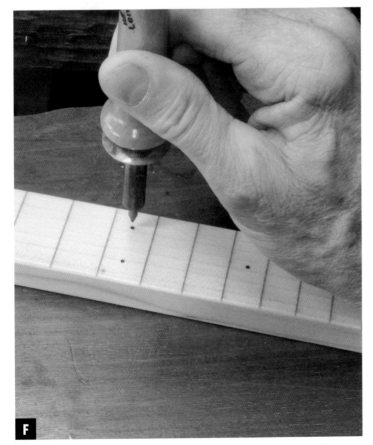

Now that the fret finger positions have been located, use a woodburner to mark them.

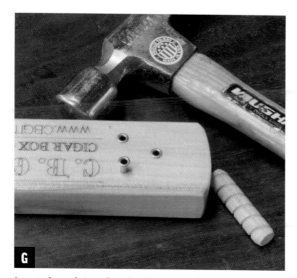

G

Insert the tailpiece ferrules by tapping them into the neck.

H

Insert the ferrules into the peghead by tapping lightly with a hammer.

INSERT FERRULES AND PARTS

While many guitars and ukuleles have designs that attach their strings using either a steel tailpiece or bridge, the kit guitar uses holes at the lower end of the neck and brass ferrules to keep the strings from digging gradually into the soft wood. Use a hammer and dowel to tap these into place **(G)**. The dowel keeps the hammer from damaging the brass.

Ferrules are also used at the head of the neck for the tuners to pass through. These must be hammered into the holes provided **(H)**. The small dowel between the face of the hammer and the ferrule keeps the ferrule from being damaged as it is driven into place.

Use the screws provided to attach the tuners **(I)**. In this soft poplar, the holes are drilled in the neck to allow the screws to pass easily into the wood. On harder woods like cherry, maple, and walnut, drilling holes to exact size is very important to keep from breaking or otherwise damaging screws.

On the kit guitar, strings pass on one side or the other of a screw to position them to travel across

I

Attach the tuners to the peghead.

Attach the positioning screws into the holes marked on the peghead.

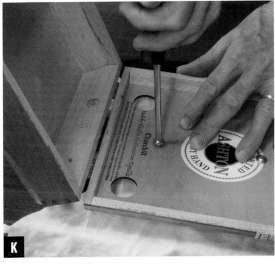

Position the cigar box and attach it.

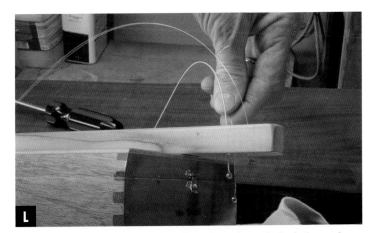

Begin stringing the guitar by threading them through the holes at the lower end of the neck.

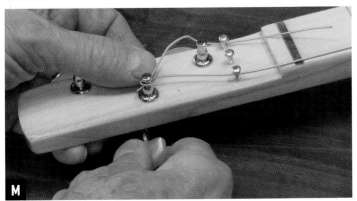

Begin tightening the strings after you pass them through the tuners.

the nut. Drive these screws partway into the holes that are already marked and drilled **(J)**.

Use the drilled holes to position the cigar box on the back side of the neck **(K)**.

Pass the strings through the ferrules at the lower end of the neck so they can begin their journey across the bridge and nut and be wound on the tuners **(L)**.

Begin tightening the strings. Pass each string through its tuning peg and begin tightening it **(M)**. The tuner on the left of the neck should wind in a counter-clockwise manner so the string passes on the outside of the screw. The tuners on the left are wound in a clockwise manner so the strings pass on the appropriate side of the guide screws as shown.

COMPLETE THE GUITAR

After the strings are loosely in place, the nut can be placed in position **(N)**.

Position the bridge as shown, and at the point indicated on the neck **(O)**. Just in case you've erased that mark in sanding, the dimension between the nut and the bridge is 25 inches (64cm).

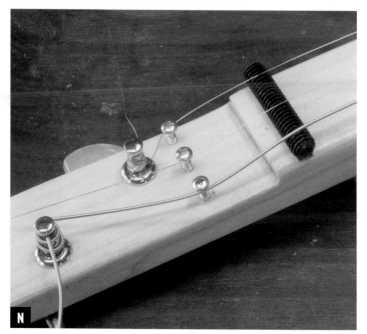

Place the nut under the strings as shown.

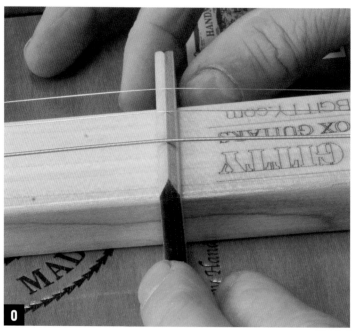

Place the bridge under the strings as shown.

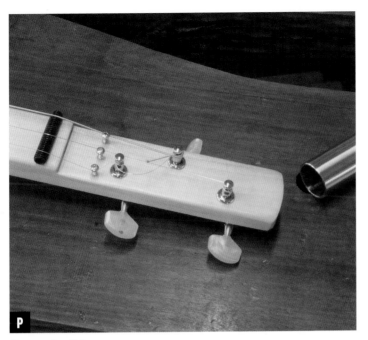

Get out the slide.

With stringing complete, get out the slide provided and you are ready to play **(P)**.

Review the look of your finished guitar **(Q)**. If ignoring the finer points of sanding and finish on the neck, you can be playing your box guitar in an hour or less, unless you are lured to a more creative approach.

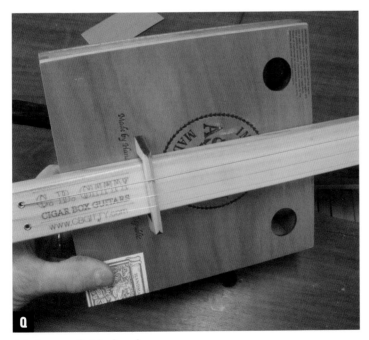

Admire your finished work.

BOX SIDES

The box on a guitar simply serves as a resonator, increasing the volume of the sound that comes from the vibrations of the strings. A completed box will have a top and bottom end, sides, and a top and back plate. This chapter focuses on the top, bottom, and sides. The top and back are added in chapter 5 (page 65).

Making a box guitar can start with a cigar box from your local tobacconist or purchased online, or you can get even more creative by making your own box. In my own case, I'm a box maker whose father died of lung cancer. Supporting an industry with which I'm not 100% aligned makes less sense for me and offers less creative opportunity than using a box I've made from scratch: You can make your box from hardwoods or soft; use nails and glue, or a more complex joinery technique; and best of all, you can choose the shape you like. While making a box from scratch takes a bit more time than using a box recently emptied of cigars, there is meaning in saying, "I made this myself," and it's healthier too, than saying, "Yes, I smoked those all myself."

In this chapter, I show a variety of ways to make a box. Some involve techniques that I've demonstrated in my other books on box making. Some of the techniques are based on what I've learned making boxes (and box guitars) with my students grades 1 through 12 at the Clear Spring School. Whether you choose to work on an easy box assembled with nails, or a more complex assembly using fine hardwoods, there will be no lack of pleasure in your finished guitar.

TOOLS & MATERIALS

Wood of choice (see text above for suggestions)	Glue	Compound miter saw or Japanese dozuki saw	C clamps	Wax paper
Tablesaw	Nails	Stop blocks	Pencil	Miter sled for tablesaw
Bandsaw	Hammer	Painter's tape	Square or angle gauge	Thin-kerf ripping blade for tablesaw
Push stick	Self-adhesive sandpaper on a board	Brad nails or pin nailer	Rubber bands	Bar clamps
Stop block			Sliding box for tablesaw fence	

PREPARE YOUR STOCK

You can get the necessary materials for making box sides by ripping hardwood or softwood stock on the tablesaw **(A)**. Any number of woods may be used, depending on whether your finished guitar will be painted or whether you plan to use the natural colors of the wood to make your guitar distinctive and interesting. Basswood or pine are perfect for painted boxes; walnut and cherry work well for boxes where the natural colors of the wood are the focal point.

MAKE A NAILED-TOGETHER BOX

For a nailed-together box, basswood or pine works best. Attaching thin sides to a thicker top and bottom end offers less likelihood of splitting the wood. Having a thicker top end gives firm structure for attaching the neck, and a tail end slightly thicker than the sides gives strength to the attachment of the tailpiece later in your guitar making procedure (chapter 8). Use glue and nails to attach the box sides to the ends **(B)**. Be careful that the edges are aligned, as this will help to reduce sanding. On the other hand, if you are looking for a more rustic look, edges that are misaligned may help to make your guitar match what you have in mind, as long as the top and back edges are aligned closely enough to glue your back and front in place later (chapter 5). The assembled box is shown here **(C)**.

Even out the edges and sand the top and bottom of the guitar box flush with self-adhesive sandpaper stuck to a board. This keeps edges crisp and square. Regardless of the type or shape of box you're making, this is part of the process before the guitar top and back are added **(D)**.

Resaw stock for box sides using the tablesaw or bandsaw. Have a push stick ready to guide the stock through the cut.

Use nails and glue to assemble the box. Spread the glue first, then position the stock and drive the nails in place.

Use thicker stock where the neck will be attached to the body of the box.

After the box is firmly nailed and glued, sand the edges flat on a sanding board covered with self-adhesive sandpaper.

MAKE SHAPED BOXES

Once you've mastered making a simple box, you can go crazy on shape. There are options shown here: a tapered box in which the bottom end is wider than where the neck is attached; a box called a "scissor-tail" that attempts to capture the wilder days of rock and roll; and a "K-body," the shape of which rests comfortably on the knee like a more common real guitar. Each of these offers some challenge over making a simple rectilinear box, but can be accomplished with a few hand and power tools.

Make a Tapered Box

Let's start with a tapered box. This is just a step away from a straight-cornered rectangle, and will help you learn the basics of changing the angles of corners. Be sure to reference the illustrations on page 156.

Cut the Sides

Use a compound miter saw to cut the angles required on the sides and bottom end first. The top end will need to be cut to final length after the sides and bottom end have been taped together.

You can cut the sides of this box with a compound miter saw or a Japanese dozuki saw. If you plan to use hand tools, be sure to very carefully mark everything prior to your first cut. The easier choice for most woodworkers these days is to use a compound miter saw because it can dial in on the perfect angle. To get the best results, use a saw with a backing board that allows stop blocks to be clamped in place to guarantee perfect lengths of stock. The compound miter saw is commonly used by home craftsmen and finish carpenters to make quick cuts, but it does its best work both in safety and accuracy of cut when a slower approach is made.

Set the angle of the saw to make your first cuts. Lower the saw into the cut after you turn it on and allow it to come up to full speed **(E)**. Release the trigger to turn off the saw when you reach the bottom of the cut. Do not lift the saw from the cut until after it has come to a complete stop **(F)**. This prevents cutting the stock a second time on the upward stroke, but most importantly, prevents the blade from lifting the cut piece and jamming it dangerously against the stop block.

Prepare for Assembly

Use tape to secure the sides to the bottom end piece so that the angled joints are held tight and secure **(G)**. With the sides secured temporarily to the bottom end, measure for the fitting of the top end **(H)**.

A compound miter saw is a useful tool to make cuts when used with a stop block. Lower the saw into the cut.

Allow the saw to come to a complete stop before raising it from the cut. Lifting the blade while spinning will engage the teeth a second time and destroy your workpiece.

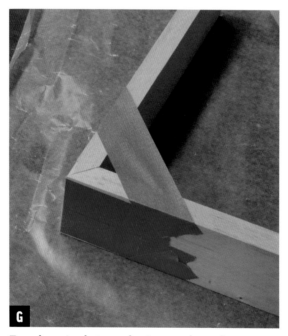

To make a simple tapered guitar, cut the angles on each end of the box sides and prepare for assembly by taping the sides to the bottom end of the guitar. Tape is sufficient to hold the parts in shape for the next step.

Measure the required length of the top piece and then cut it to length.

When the parts have been cut to the right length and angle, the miters should fit tightly, with no visible openings in the joints.

Use tape at all corners but one, as you begin spreading glue in each joint.

Tape each joint and wait for the glue to set before using brad nails or a pin nailer to strengthen each joint. A block of hardwood will be glued in place later to strengthen the attachment of the neck.

The angles of the cut are already predetermined and should have been set when you cut the sides to length. Check the fit of the corners. At this point, each joint should close tightly using tape alone to hold the parts together **(I)**. When you are satisfied with the fit of the parts, open the assembled parts at one joint, lay the pieces out flat in a row, and apply glue to each joint **(J)**. With well-cut joints, glue and tape alone should hold the box sides together as the glue sets **(K)**. Add additional hardwood blocking in the upper end of the box to strengthen where the neck is attached. After the glue has set, brad nails or pins can be added for additional strength. Use a board with self-adhesive sandpaper to flatten the edges and where the top and back will be glued in place.

Make a K-Body

The K-body guitar gets its name from its shape. In addition to being comfortable to rest on your knee, it is also relatively easy to make using the following steps. Be sure to reference the illustrations on page 157.

Cut the Sides

Use the compound miter saw to cut the pieces to the correct angle, but leave each piece about an extra inch (25mm) in length for trimming to an exact fit later **(L).** Cut an extra piece to the same angle used to form the K side but only about ¾ to 1 inch (19 to 25mm) in length, and glue it in place as shown **(M).**

Assemble the K

Use small ⅞-inch (22mm)-long nails to assemble the K side **(N).** Starting the nails in the wood first is much easier than holding the parts in the right position and getting the nails started at the same time. Apply glue to the joint **(O).** Use a small hammer to drive the nails into place **(P).** Set aside the K assembly as the glue dries.

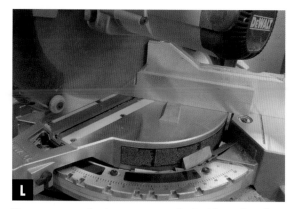

L

Use a compound miter saw to cut the inside angles of the K.

M

Glue and clamp an extra angle piece to one end of the angled piece.

N

Position and tack the nails partway in place to prepare for the first step in assembly.

O

Apply glue to both sides of the joint.

P

Nail the other end of the K in place.

Form a rabbet on the end of the top and bottom pieces of the guitar body that will intersect with the straight side.

Use glue and nails to attach the pieces to the straight side of the guitar body.

Hold the K side of the guitar in place to mark the necessary angles on the side, top, and bottom assembly.

Prepare the Top and Bottom Ends

To hold the top and bottom ends of the guitar square, first cut a rabbet joint at one end of each piece where they will intersect with the straight side. This joint provides additional surface area for gluing, but also aids in aligning the edges where the top and bottom are aligned with the sides. This same joint will be used later in this chapter to made a walnut-sided box (page 31). Set a stop block on the tablesaw and set the blade height so that ⅛-inch (3mm) of material is left on the top side of the stock (Q). When you glue and nail this joint, you will see the advantages in making a strong box for the K-body guitar (R).

Complete the Top and Bottom Ends

With the top and bottom ends of the guitar nailed in place, you can position the K side on top to mark the angles where you will need to cut (S). These cuts can be made with a dozuki saw or the compound miter saw. If using hand tools, first mark your cut line with a square so that you can follow the line precisely with the saw (T).

Mark the top and bottom for cutting with hand tools.

Use the dozuki saw to make the cut (U). If you plan to cut with a compound miter saw, determine the angle of the cut and set the saw to cut at the same angle. Use an angle gauge to measure; note that the angle at the top and the angle at the bottom will be different angles and require separate settings of the saw (V). Use the compound miter saw to cut the top and bottom end pieces to the correct angle and length (W).

Assemble the Pieces

Mark the length of the K side of the guitar box and trim it to the right length and angle at each end, leaving a bit of extra length at each to be trimmed after assembly (X).

Use a dozuki saw to cut the top and bottom to fit the K side.

If you prefer to use power tools, use an angle gauge to determine the angles where the K side fits the top and bottom of the assembly.

Use a compound miter saw to cut the top and bottom pieces to the right length and angle.

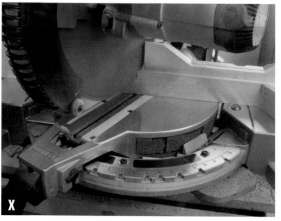

Use the compound miter saw to cut the K side to length, leaving it about ¼-inch long at each end.

Use rubber bands to hold the K side in place as the glue dries.

Use ⅞-inch-long nails to hold the K side to the top and bottom of the guitar box.

Clamp the hardwood block in place as the glue sets.

Apply glue to the joints; use rubber bands to hold the assembly together as the glue sets **(Y)**. After the glue has set, use small nails to add greater strength to the joints **(Z)**. Add hardwood blocking to the inside top and bottom of the guitar box to provide for securely attaching the neck. Spread glue first, then use clamps to hold the block in place **(AA)**.

Make a Scissor-Tail

This scissor-tail design features a rock-and-rock look. Making a scissor-tail guitar is more difficult; the acute angles required to make the pointed ends are a bit more of a challenge. Be sure to reference the illustrations on page 159.

Cut the First Angles

Use a sliding box on the tablesaw fence to assist with this cut because the cuts required are out of range for the tilt of the tablesaw, and equally out of range for the compound miter saw. The sliding box on the tablesaw fence allows the stock to be held vertically during the cut. Clamp the stock to the sliding box and use the tablesaw with the blade tilted to 15°. Four pieces will be cut at this angle for one guitar **(BB)**.

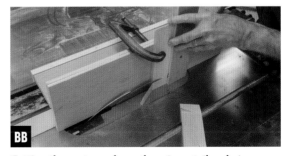

Cutting the acute angle on the scissor-tail end pieces requires a sliding guide that holds the pieces vertical as they slide through the angle cut.

The angle where the two tails come together is a common 90° joint and can be formed either on the tablesaw with sled, or using the compound miter saw set at 45°. Use tape and glue to begin the assembly of the scissor-tail box **(CC).** Wax paper is a great tool to keep a guitar body from getting glued to the bench.

Complete the Assembly

When the glue has dried, use an angle gauge to find the necessary angle for cutting the top end piece to length. Note that one end of the top end piece will be cut at 90° and the other end will be determined with the angle gauge **(DD).** Note that using an extra-thick piece of hardwood as the upper end of the guitar body as seen here allows for the attachment of the neck without gluing additional blocking in place. After cutting the top, do a trial assembly of the box **(EE).**

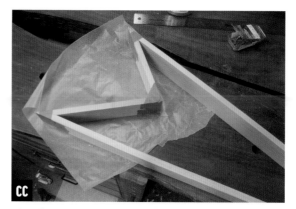

Glue the pieces together to begin forming the body of the scissor-tail guitar.

Use an angle gauge to determine the angle for the top end to fit. Use a block at the 90° side to make sure the angle gauge is accurate.

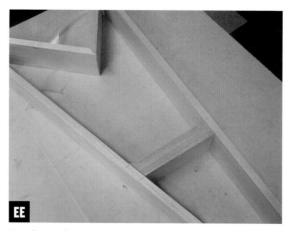

Cut the angle at one end of the top piece, and then a 90° cut at the other. The piece can be moved up or down the length of the body to find a perfect fit.

FF

Use tape to hold the parts together as the glue sets.

GG

After the final shape is achieved, use a pin nailer to strengthen each joint.

HH

To make a box from finer hardwood like this walnut, first cut a rabbet joint at the corners to allow the parts to nest tightly together.

Note that the sides are a bit long so they can be cut to final length after final assembly. Apply glue to the upper end piece and use tape to hold the part in place as the glue sets (**FF**). Trim the extra length from the scissor tail sides and then use a pin nailer to add additional strength to the joints (**GG**).

MAKE A HARDWOOD BOX

Making hardwood-bodied box guitars offers the box maker an opportunity to make a beautiful guitar. For the guitar maker, the techniques used in making fine hardwood boxes may make things much easier than is the case with a conventional guitar. Box makers will find it irresistible to apply conventional fine box making techniques in making box guitars.

The first step is to plane the materials for the sides and top and bottom ends. Use thicker wood for the top end, as that's where the neck will be attached, and slightly thicker wood at the bottom end, as that's where the tailpiece will be screwed in place. Another option is to simply glue additional blocking in place, as done in making the K-body guitar. Next is the creation of rabbet joints. Use a stop block to control the cuts. Carefully set the blade height so that it is about ⅛-inch (3mm) shy of cutting all the way through. Move the sled back and forth with the workpiece passing over the blade; each cut brings the end of the stock closer to the stop block. When the workpiece is firmly against the stop block, the rabbet joint will be fully formed (**HH**).

Spread glue in the rabbets on both ends of the top and bottom end stock as you prepare for assembly **(II).** Finally, use rubber bands to hold the parts tight as the glue sets **(JJ).** The amount of surface area that is glued in assembly of this box gives it strength, particularly when the top and back of the guitar are glued in place.

MAKE A KEYED MITER BOX

Box makers often debate whether the keyed miter joint adds strength to a box or if it simply makes it more beautiful through the use of contrasting keys. Of course, there is also the opinion that this joint does both things.

Cut the Four Sides

Use a miter sled on the tablesaw to begin cutting the joints required for this box. The miter sled is used with the blade tilted and carefully set at 45°. A stop block is used to make certain that opposite parts are cut at exactly the same length. Use a spacer block on the sled that can be removed or replaced so that cuts can be made in an

Apply glue to both the joints.

Use rubber bands to hold the parts together as the glue sets.

Make a fancy box with contrasting miter keys by first cutting mitered corners on the tablesaw.

To offset the length from the width of the box, the long parts are cut with just the stop block, and a 2-inch spacer block is used against the stop block for the shorter parts.

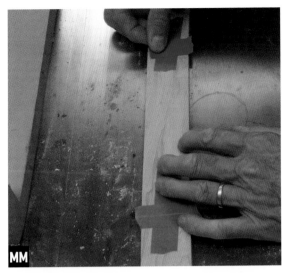

Use tape to connect the mitered ends of the stock.

Glue and clamp the sides of the box and wait until the glue sets.

Use a keyed miter guide to cut the grooves at each corner for the miter keys to fit.

alternating fashion and matching grain around the sides can be perfected. For each piece, a trimming cut must be made face down on the sled, followed by a second cut face up with one end against the stop block. Cut your first piece to form a box side using the sled with spacer block removed **(KK).**

Cut the second piece, which will become either the top or bottom end of the box. This is done with the spacer block added between the piece and the stop block **(LL).** The third cut is then make with the spacer block removed, and the final piece is cut with the spacer block back in place. It may be a challenge for beginners to understand this technique; it requires practice, but there is a useful rhythm to it.

Assemble the Sides

When the four sides of the box have been cut, carefully align the edges and tape the parts end to end in preparation for assembly **(MM).** Spread glue on the mitered surfaces and roll the four sides into a box. Use corner clamps, tape, or large rubber bands to hold the four sides in shape as the glue dries **(NN).**

Add the Miter Keys

Use a shopmade jig on the tablesaw to guide the box corners for cutting the grooves for the miter keys to fit (see illustrations on page 160). The jig simply holds the box vertically and at a 45° angle as it passes across the tablesaw blade, which is set at a specific height so that it does not cut all the way through into the inside of the box **(OO).** Thin-kerf ripping blades have a flat top grind, which allows the keys to fit tightly into the grooves.

Using the tablesaw, rip thin strips of contrasting wood, and then tape them into a bundle before cutting them into triangle shapes using the miter sled on the tablesaw. Spread just a bit of glue in each groove and wipe a small amount on each key before pushing it into place **(PP).** Keep a tack hammer handy to tap any recalcitrant keys, but if a key appears too tight, requiring more than a modest amount of effort to install in the groove, simply throw it away and use another. A light sanding of keys is sometimes required for a good fit.

Add additional blocking to one end for attaching the neck after you've finished assembly of the box **(QQ).**

Sand the Keys

Before sanding, use the bandsaw to cut the keys almost flush with the box sides. A low fence is helpful to hold the box sides far enough from the blade that the blade cannot mar the sides **(RR).** Use self-adhesive sandpaper on a flat board to sand the keys smooth and flush to the sides of the box **(SS).** The finished keyed miter joint is a sign of craftsmanship when used in making a box guitar **(TT).**

Cut ⅛-inch-thick keys and glue them in place to strengthen the joints.

Add thickness and strength to the top end of the guitar box by gluing and clamping a hardwood block in place.

Use the bandsaw to trim the miter keys almost flush to the sides of the box.

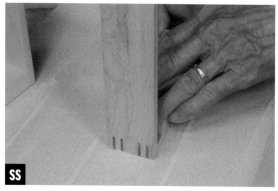

Sand the keys flush with the sides of the box.

The keyed miter joint adds a touch of elegant craftsmanship to your guitar.

MAKE A KIT-STYLE BOX BODY

Making a simple wooden box like a cigar box is quite easy using the techniques shown in this book. Because a kit guitar, or one reliant on a cigar box as its origin, can open and close on hinges, it can be screwed easily to a full-length neck.

Build a box in two parts.
You'll need a set of box sides for the lid and a set for the base. Make them the same dimensions so that one will close tight to the other.

Make the top and back.
Cut Baltic birch plywood to serve as a top and back, and use brads and glue to hold the parts in place.

Install the hinges.
Screw on the hinges; or, if you want to avoid such complications, simply glue the parts of your box together, lid to base, after the neck is installed.

Install a hasp.
If you want to be able to open and close your box to store things inside or to add electronics, use a small brass hasp as a lock. The one shown simply nails in place.

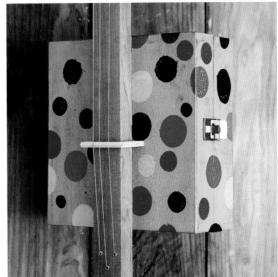

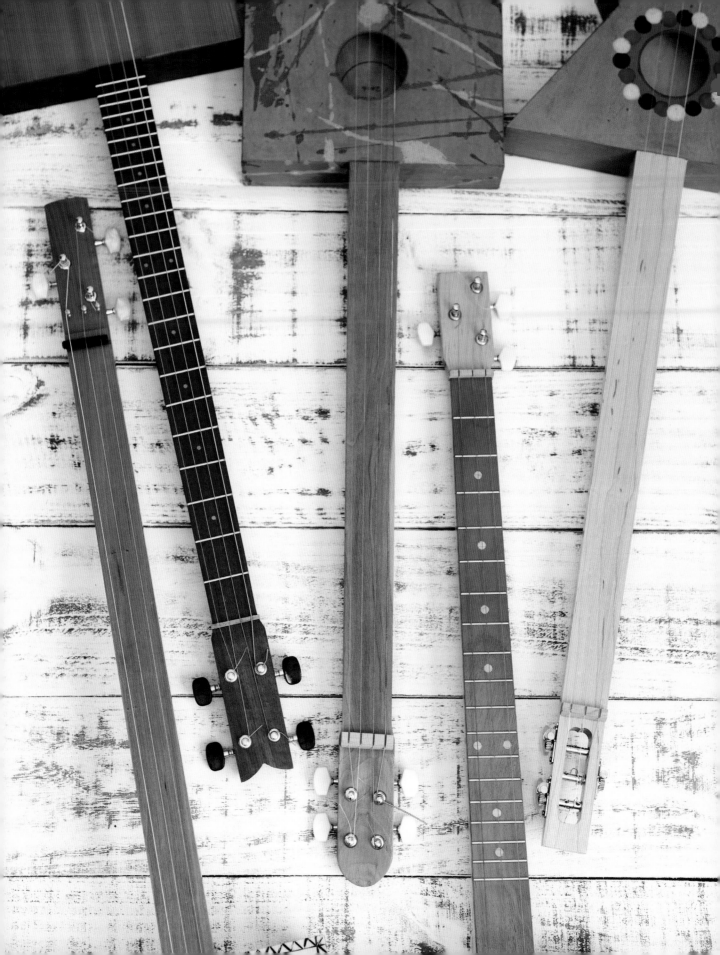

Chapter 3

NECKS

Here you'll see three different proven types of necks for box guitars. If you choose to make these out of hardwoods, you'll increase the strength and longevity of your guitar. Using cherry, maple, and walnut, the necks are relatively inexpensive to make, and you can choose the level of complexity to match the tools you have available and the level of handwork you are interested in using to make your guitar.

The simplest approach to use in making a neck for a box guitar follows the approach used by a kit guitar. Choose hardwood ¾-inch (19mm) thick, saw it to width and length, and then form a lower section at the top end for mounting the tuners. Be sure to reference the illustrations on pages 161–162.

TOOLS & MATERIALS

Wood of choice	Straightedge	Random orbit sander or sanding block	Fine rasp	Chisel
Planer	Square		Sandpaper	Spindle sander or dowel with sandpaper
Tablesaw	Tape measure	Glue	Drill or drill press with drill bits	
Jointer	Bandsaw	C clamps	Screws	Router table with roundover bit
Push block	Hand plane	Coarse rasp	Marking gauge	
Pencil				

A

Prepare the neck by planing and cutting it out with a tablesaw.

B

Cut the tuning peg area.

C

Complete the tuning peg area by removing the thin piece of wood at the top of the neck.

FLAT PEGHEAD

Most guitar necks start out in the same manner: planing and then cutting on a tablesaw **(A)**. Join one edge flat on the jointer, then set the fence to rip your stock at your intended width. Have a push block handy to safely finish the cut, keeping your hands a safe distance from the blade. This piece is ¾-inch (19mm) thick and ripped to a width of 1½ inches (38mm).

Use a bandsaw with fence to cut into the end of the neck where the tuning pegs will fit **(B)**.

Use the sled on the tablesaw to remove the thin piece of wood at the top end of the neck formed in the last step **(C)**. Use a stop block to control the length of the cut.

Make a shallow saw cut (¹⁄₁₆-inch [2mm]) to mark the spot where the nut will fit **(D)**.

Use a sander to flatten the area where the tuners will fit **(E)**. As an alternative to a power sander, consider a sanding block. You could also leave it relatively coarse for a more rustic effect.

D

Mark the nut placement with a light cut.

E

Flatten the tuner area with a sander.

Prepare the neck by planing and cutting it out with a tablesaw.

Mark the neck to prepare for shaping.

Cut the underside taper of the neck.

ANGLED PEGHEAD

Plane the stock and cut out the neck using a tablesaw **(A)**.

You have a choice of leaving the stock square if making a kit-style neck, or shaping it to fit your hand. Mark the shape of the neck using a straightedge, square, tape measure, and pencil **(B)**. It should taper from the end to the peghead, expanding back to full width where the tuning pegs will be installed.

Use a bandsaw to cut the underside of the neck to its slightly tapered shape **(C)**.

ANGLED PEGHEAD, *continued*

Cut the side tapers of the neck.

Flatten the sides and back.

Use the bandsaw to taper each side of the neck and form the peghead **(D)**.

Use a plane to flatten and smooth the back and sides of the neck **(E)**.

Plane the neck's edges, being careful to keep the sides straight and flat **(F)**.

Plane the edges of the neck.

Thicken both ends of the neck by gluing on blocks.

Start to form the peghed with the bandsaw.

Use the bandsaw to cut the underside of the peghead.

Glue blocks on both ends to thicken the peghead and where the neck attaches to the box body **(G)**.

Make a bandsaw cut to begin forming the peghead **(H)**. This is a straight cut, forming an angled plane where the tuning pegs can be mounted lower than the nut.

Use the fence on the bandsaw and make a straight cut to begin forming the underside of the peghead **(I)**.

ANGLED PEGHEAD, *continued*

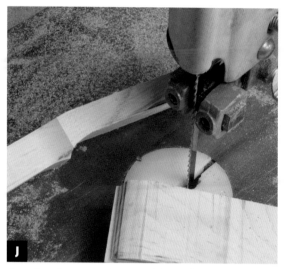

J

Complete the rough shaping of the neck with a curving cut.

K

Prepare to rasp by marking the underside of the neck.

Remove the fence and make a curving cut to finish the underside of the peghead **(J).** Once the waste is removed, the shape of the peghead is revealed. The underside can be sanded flat and smooth with sanding blocks.

Use a pencil to mark on the underside of the neck to prepare for shaping with a rasp **(K).** Hold the pencil so that its tip protrudes about ½ inch (13mm) from your index finger and mark along the sides and underside of the neck.

Continue the marks on each side **(L).**

L

Complete the marking of the neck on both sides.

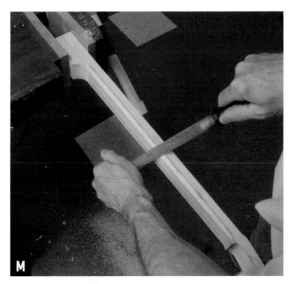

Begin rasping with a coarse rasp.

Continue to round the underside of the neck with the rasp.

Switch to a finer rasp to complete rasping.

Use a coarse rasp to begin rounding the edges of the underside of the neck (**M**). If you create a flat spot first between the marked lines, the rest of the rounding will come easy.

Gently round the underside from one end to the other, using your pencil marks to guide where you need to rasp next (**N**).

Use a finer rasp to continue rounding the underside of the neck (**O**).

Use sandpaper to finish shaping and smoothing the neck (**P**).

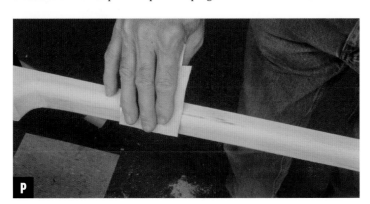

Sand the neck to finish smoothing it.

ANGLED PEGHEAD, *continued*

Shape the end of the neck and finish with sandpaper.

Flatten the peghead with a plane.

Shape and sand the end of the neck where it will be attached to the body of the box guitar **(Q).**

Use a plane to flatten where the tuning pegs will be installed **(R).**

Create an interesting shape on the end of the peghead **(S).** This one, being formed in a walnut neck, is but one of many choices. Design in pencil first, then cut. After cutting, use sanding blocks to finish shaping.

Design the peghead to add visual interest.

Prepare to taper the blank with the jointer.

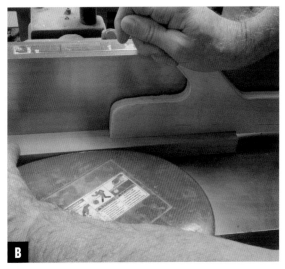

Taper the blank on three sides.

Square the top of the neck with a saw.

SIMPLE MACHINED NECK

To make a simple machined hardwood neck, start with the jointer and taper your hardwood blank by placing one end on the outfeed table **(A).** The jointer must be running as the stock is lowered into the cut. This requires a firm grip on the wood and that the hands be well away from the cutter head.

Hold the stock firmly as you turn on the jointer, and using a push block to maintain a good grip, guide the stock through the cut on three sides **(B).** This will give you a neck that tapers gently toward the top.

Use the compound miter saw or tablesaw sled to trim the top end of the neck square **(C).**

SIMPLE MACHINED NECK, *continued*

Drill the tuner recess with a drill press.

Complete the tuner recess using a chisel.

Use the drill press or hand-held power drill to drill holes where the tuners will fit **(D).** This is a slotted tuner head.

Use a marking gauge to scribe a cut line on either side of the holes and use a chisel to remove the material left between **(E).**

Cut a block of wood to strengthen the mounting end of the neck and glue it in place **(F).**

Attach a block to the mounting end of the neck.

Round the neck's end.

Smooth the neck's end with a spindle sander.

Round the neck's edges with a router.

Use the bandsaw to cut the lower end of the neck to a more pleasing shape **(G)**.

Use a spindle sander to smooth the bandsaw cut or leave it rough for a more rustic appearance **(H)**. Hand-held rasps, sanding blocks, or a sheet of sandpaper wrapped around a large dowel can also be used to sand the junction smooth.

Use a roundover bit in the router table as an easy way to smooth the underside of the neck, making it more comfortable to play **(I)**.

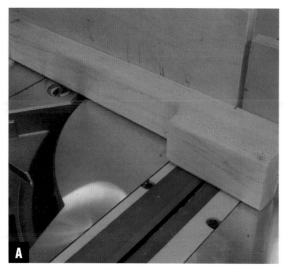

A

Cut the neck to length with a compound miter saw.

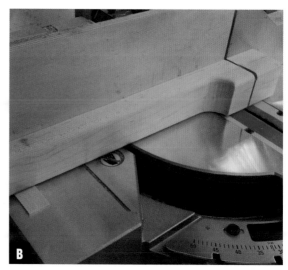

B

Prepare to drill.

COMPLETE THE NECK

After you have created your neck of choice, proceed with these steps to attach it to the box.

Use a compound miter saw to cut the neck to length. The end where the neck will be attached to the body of the box should be about 3 inches (76mm) long so that sufficiently sized screws can be used to attach the two parts. Note the small shim used to hold the neck square on the saw **(A).** A combination square should be used to check that it is so. Hold the stock tight to the saw as you square the end of the neck and cut it to length.

The finished neck is ready to drill for attachment to the body of the box **(B).**

Drill a pilot hole for a screw to attach the box body to the neck **(C).** Center the pilot hole between the two sides of the neck and ¾ inch (19mm) down from the top side.

C

Drill a pilot hole in the neck to attach the box body.

Drill a pilot hole in the box body.

Drill a second hole to stabilize.

If needed, strengthen the box with blocking.

Drill a matching hole in the body of the box ½-inch (13mm) down from the top edge **(D)**. If planning to use an attached fretboard, drill the pilot hole ⅝-inch (16mm) down from the top edge so the neck and the ⅛-inch (3mm)-thick top will be flush.

In order to keep the neck from twisting in relation to the body of the box, use a second, shorter screw below the first **(E)**. This hole must be piloted and countersunk to keep from splitting your carefully crafted neck.

Where necessary, such as when using thinner stock or softwoods to build the body of the box, use hardwood blocking to strengthen the attachment of the neck **(F)**.

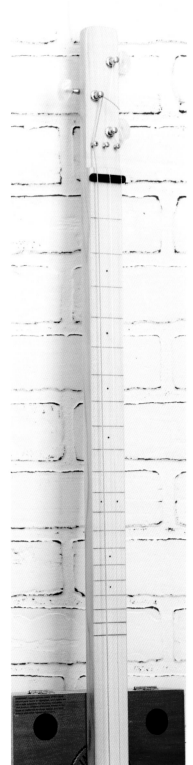

Chapter 4

FRETS

Many instruments, like violins and string bass, are fretless and dependent on experienced fingers finding just the right note. Like those instruments, many box guitars (including the kit in this book on page 11) are made either completely without frets or with drawn-on frets only and can be played with a slide.

Box guitars can also be made with frets, and for many musicians, added pleasure may come from playing just the right notes. Frets also offer the opportunity for playing chords, even on a three- or four-string guitar. To add frets is actually quite easy using a template for marking their precise locations and a fret saw for cutting the tiny grooves for them to fit.

The frets can be sawn directly into the guitar neck or a thin wooden fretboard can be added to the finished neck. In either case, the process is nearly the same. Or, if you prefer to avoid such efforts on a first guitar, fretboards and entire pre-fretted necks can be ordered online.

TOOLS & MATERIALS

Fretboard stock or guitar neck	Fret saw with built-in or homemade depth guide	Contrasting wood scraps	Sanding block or hand plane
Fret template or placement tool of choice	Fret wire	Glue	Scrap block of wood
Clamp	Drill press with ¼-inch (6mm) drill bit and ¼-inch (6mm) plug cutter	Hammer	Wire cutters
Pencil		Sandpaper	Self-adhesive sandpaper on flat board
		Bandsaw	Bar clamps

LAYING OUT FRET MEASUREMENTS

You have a few choices when it comes to determining fret placement. If laying out your own fret measurements, the usual manner is to make your measurements from the position of the nut, and to make every measurement from that point rather than measuring one fret position from the last—a technique that would build in cumulative error. It is easy to use online fret calculation tools to determine fret positions for any given distance between bridge and nut. You simply tell the calculator the distance from nut to bridge and then mark those measurements on your neck or fretboard.

Of course, the easier way is to avoid the math and the accurate measurements required in laying out frets, and rely instead on a template accurately made for that purpose. I chose a template from C.B. Gitty that is designed for a distance between nut and bridge of 24¾ inches (63cm). Templates of this type are extremely accurate and easy to use. This template is intended for box guitars, but will also work for a six-string if you simply extend your pencil marks to the full width of the neck or fretboard.

Prepare your fretboard stock to overlay the front of the guitar and make sure the neck is flush to the guitar top so they can be successfully glued.

Clamp the template to the fretboard and use a pencil to indicate proper positions for each fret. This marking template also shows the correct positions for the dots that can be inlaid at the proper fret marking positions.

Remove the marking template and the grooves for your frets to fit are ready to saw.

FRETBOARDS VERSUS NECKS

Frets can be added to fretboards or directly to the neck of a guitar. These steps are all shown on a fretboard. If adding a fretboard, plan your neck so that its face attaches flush with the body of the box. This will allow your fretboard to extend down slightly over the front of the guitar while laying flat on both **(A).** It should also fit the neck widthwise. This thin fretboard is made from mahogany, but any number of other hardwoods will do. If planning a painted finish, you will want to wait to glue on the fretboard until after the paint is dry.

MARK THE FRETS

Mark the fret placement using your desired method. The fretboard should be long enough at this point that it can be effectively clamped at each end. Plan to cut it at the nut and to final length after the fret grooves have been cut. For this example, a template is shown. Clamp the template onto the fretboard. Use a sharp pencil to mark the location of each fret and the nut **(B).** The fretboard, when marked, will show the positions of each fret as well as the positions of the inlaid dots marking the 3rd, 5th, 7th, 9th, 12th, 15th, 17th, and 19th frets **(C).**

CUT THE FRETS

Use a fret saw to cut the grooves for the frets to fit **(D)**. Fret wire comes in specific sizes and has small barbs that lock it in place. The saw you use must be sized to fit the fret wire you have selected. Each fret groove must also be cut to an adequate depth, so to make cutting to the precise depth easier, add a small piece of wood to the fret saw held in place with rare earth magnets **(E)**. Design this piece to fit against the frame of the fret saw, leaving just the right amount of cutting edge exposed. As an alternative, you can purchase a fret saw with adjustable depth stop. Either method allows you to observe the proper depth, but also make certain that the grooves are not too deep and are of even depth across the width of the fretboard **(F)**. Carefully observe that all fret grooves are cut to an adequate depth **(G)**.

Use a fret saw to make each cut, working systematically from one end to the other.

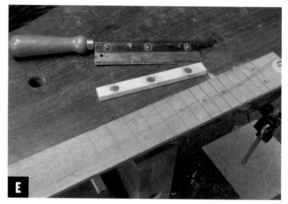

A depth guide using rare earth magnets can be made to keep your fret saw cutting to exactly the right depth.

It requires concentration to keep on the line, but the depth stop helps to make certain each fret groove is deep enough and not too deep.

Once cut, check all the grooves to make certain they are of uniform depth.

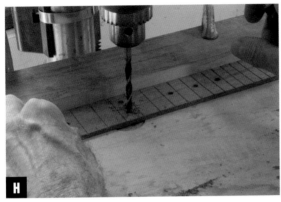

Use the drill press to drill holes for the inlaid dots to fit. Use a fence on the drill press to make certain the inlays are perfectly centered and aligned.

Use a plug cutter to make inlay dots from a contrasting wood. These are maple.

Apply a bit of glue in each hole and tap a dot in place, taking care that the grain in each dot runs the same direction. The grain can run parallel or perpendicular to the grain in the fretboard—the particular direction doesn't matter, but overall consistency does.

ADD THE INLAID DOTS

To add the inlaid dots to a fretboard, set up the drill press with a ¼-inch (6mm) drill bit and set the depth so it goes only about ¼-inch (6mm) into the face of the fretboard. Use a fence to control the distance of each inlaid dot from the edge, and to make certain that the dots down the center of the fretboard are at the center **(H)**.

Make wooden dots of a contrasting wood by using a ¼-inch (6mm) plug cutter in the drill press **(I)**. Apply glue in the holes in the fretboard, tap the plugs in place, and sand them flush with the face of the fretboard **(J)**. Make sure all the grain of the plugs is facing the same direction.

TRIM THE FRETBOARD

When the fret grooves are cut, and the inlaid dots are in place, cut the fretboard to length. First cut it off where the nut will fit, and then cut it at the other end to fit with the design of your guitar. Use clamps to secure the fretboard to the neck so you can mark it for trimming to width **(K)**.

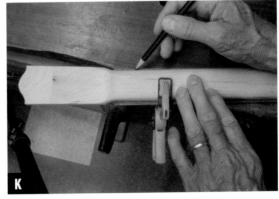

Once the fretboard has been sanded flush, clamp the fretboard and neck together to trace the shape of one to the other.

Use a bandsaw to trim the width and cut just outside the line **(L)**. Leave a bit to be cleaned up during assembly. Use a block plane to even the edges of the fretboard for gluing to the neck **(M)**.

INSTALL THE FRETS

To install the frets, use a block of wood to cushion and direct the force of the hammer. Fret wire comes in straight lengths, with each giving enough material for several frets. Use wire cutters to trim the frets to length as you go, leaving just a bit sticking out beyond the fretboard at each side **(N)**. When all the frets have been installed, use self-adhesive sandpaper on a flat board to sand the frets flush with the fretboard sides **(O)**.

Use the bandsaw to shape the fretboard to fit the neck.

Use a plane to clean up the band-sawn edges on both sides. Stay just outside the line so the fretboard and neck can be sanded flush after gluing.

Fret after fret, tap a length in place and trim it off with sharp nippers. Use a block of wood to spread the impact of the hammer and to direct the frets into place.

Use self-adhesive sandpaper on a board to sand the ends of the frets flush with the sides of the fretboard.

Gently sand the corners of the frets so that they feel smooth to the touch as you play.

Glue and clamp the fretboard in place on the guitar neck.

When the sides have been sanded flush, tilt the fretboard slightly to continue sanding the ends of the frets smooth **(P)**. When the frets have been sanded, use clamps and glue to secure the fretboard to the neck **(Q)**. After the glue is dry, sand down the edges of the fretboard so they transition smoothly into the neck itself.

SPECIAL CONSIDERATIONS FOR A SIX-STRING GUITAR FRETBOARD

In making a six-string guitar, the maker may be just a bit fussier about the sound due to the use of common chords during play. You can increase the accuracy of the placement of frets by using a guide block to make certain that each fret is square to the neck **(R)**. Use the marking template to mark the various locations for the frets, then use the guide block as you cut each fret groove. To make this easier, use a larger fret saw that has a built in, adjustable depth stop **(S)**. When all the fret grooves have been cut, trace the outline of the neck so that the fretboard can be trimmed to width **(T)**. Use a block of wood to cushion the hammer force as you install each fret **(U)**.

Using a guide block on the line at each fret location can help make certain each fret is square to the neck.

This saw comes with an adjustable depth guide that allows it to cut only the depth required for each fret.

When the fret grooves are all sawn, clamp the fretboard to the neck and trace it for trimming.

Hammer the fret wire into the grooves and trim each fret to length.

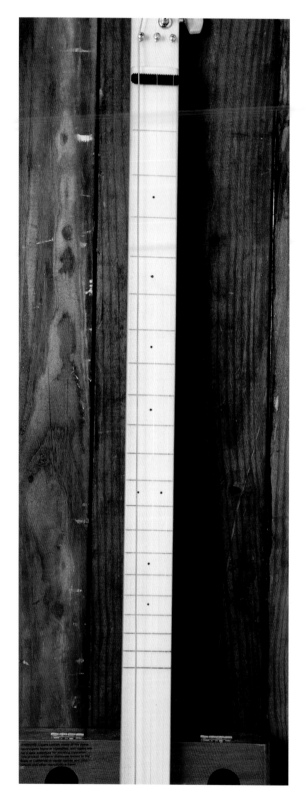

Chapter 5

TOPS *and* BACKS

The top and back of a guitar need to be strong enough to support the bridge but light enough to vibrate along with the vibrations of the strings. Some woods are more resonant than others.

Baltic birch in a ⅛-inch (3mm) thickness is available through lumber yards and big box hardware stores in sheets 5 by 5 feet (1.5 by 1.5m) or online in smaller sizes. One full sheet can make a number of guitars, and it can be used for both the top and back. While Baltic birch is not as lovely as some woods, it is ideal for guitars you plan to paint. It is available in a thickness perfect for fabricating the top and back and that makes it the perfect choice for a beginning guitar maker. In this chapter, we'll also cover resawing of woods on the tablesaw, a technique that allows the guitar maker to use a variety of woods. Resawing western cedar yields a top with pleasant tonal qualities, and various hardwoods like cherry and walnut can be used to make an attractive back.

If you are planning on electrifying your guitar, be sure to read that chapter (page 105) before attaching the back panel.

TOOLS & MATERIALS

⅛-inch (3mm)-thick Baltic birch plywood or thicker hardwood for resawing	Guitar box body of choice	Hand plane	Feather board
	Drill and Forstner bits of choice	Rasps	Bar clamps
Bandsaw, scroll saw, or coping saw		Files	Drum sander or hand plane
	Glue	Sanding block	
Pencil		Thin-kerf ripping blade	Drill press with circle cutter
	Clamps of choice		

MAKE A TOP AND BACK FROM PLYWOOD

Whether you are making a simple box shape or one of the more complex designs from chapter 2, the process of making a top and back from Baltic birch is the same. Note that it is best to attach the top and back one piece at a time so as not to rush the process.

Trace the Shape

Cut a piece slightly oversized, and trace the shape of the guitar box in pencil **(A).** To keep cutting and fitting at a minimum, align the top edge of the plywood along the top side of the guitar and tight against the neck before tracing the line. When the shape is marked clearly on the plywood, use a bandsaw, scroll saw, or coping saw to cut the shape **(B).** Be careful to stay just barely outside the line on the cuts so that when glued to the box sides, a small amount of overlap will allow you to plane and sand the edges flush to the sides. Continue cutting until the shape is formed in full **(C).**

Trace around the sides of the box to mark the plywood for sawing into a guitar top or back.

Use a bandsaw, scroll saw, or coping saw to cut just to the outside of your marked lines. Cut along the sides first.

Continue cutting the shape of the guitar.

Mark the location of the sound holes. If using multiple holes, Forstner bits may be of sufficient size to provide sufficient opening in the top.

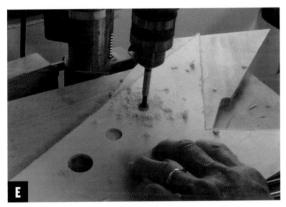

Use a drill press to drill through from the front. Be sure to have sufficient backing on the underside to prevent tearout.

Spread glue along the edge of the box body. Note the thicker hardwood at the top of the body that provides strength to the attachment of the neck.

Add Sound Holes

Before attaching the guitar top, determine where you want to make sound holes. On this guitar, three are shown, drilled with Forstner bits in descending size **(D)**. Carefully mark the location of the sound hole(s). Use the drill press to drill the sound holes **(E)**. Use scrap wood under the top to avoid tearout as you drill through.

Attach the Front

When the front is ready, spread glue along the edges of the sides of the box **(F)**. One nice thing about having the box sides made of thicker wood is that plenty of surface is provided on the edge for an effective glue joint. Use clamps to hold the top in place on the guitar box as the glue sets **(G)**.

Use lots of clamps to secure the top to the sides, and check carefully along each edge to make sure the plywood is pulled tight to the sides of the box.

Pay particular attention to the area where the top fits up to the neck, as this is a place where extra clamping pressure may be required **(H)**. Repeat the steps to produce and attach the back.

CLAMPS

It is often said of woodworkers that they never have quite enough clamps. There is another factor involved in addition to quantity: You need to have enough of certain kinds, also. In this case, I made some of my own clamps using plastic knobs, strips of wood, and 4-inch (10cm)-long ¼-inch (6mm) carriage bolts. If you prefer to avoid using so many clamps, consider using small nails to hold the top and bottom in place during gluing.

Smooth the Edges

There are a few useful tools to smooth the edges where the top and back meet the sides. A plane will quickly shave an edge down flush where there are flat surfaces where it can be used **(I)**. Inside areas where a plane will not fit can be best addressed with rasps and sanding blocks **(J, K, and L)**.

H Pay particular attention to where the top is secured to the area around the neck.

I A block plane works well to even the areas on the flat areas where it can gain access. Be careful not to plane against the grain.

J Use rasps, files, and sanding blocks to even the edges where the plane won't reach.

K Use a sanding block to sand the back even where the neck is attached.

In your use of a rasp, cut in toward the sides, and not away, as cutting out can splinter the edges.

Use the tablesaw to cut thin slices of solid wood for either the top or back. Cut in on one edge and then the other so the saw kerfs meet at the center of the stock.

Glue the edges together to make a book-matched panel.

MAKE A RESAWN TOP OR BACK

Solid wood tops and backs for guitars are usually book-matched, meaning that they are glued up to full width from matching narrow stock. Book-matching creates interesting and beautiful patterns, as the grain on one side will be perfectly symmetrical with the grain on the other.

Slice the Wood

Use the tablesaw to cut solid wood into thin slices for tops and back. You can buy top and back material online from a variety of sources, but for those with common woodworking equipment like a tablesaw or bandsaw, producing your own tops and backs is approachable. On the tablesaw, use a thin-kerf ripping blade to make best use of the original stock. Raise the blade so it cuts just barely over the halfway point. Use a feather board to hold the stock tight to the fence **(M).** After the first cut is made, turn the stock end for end, keeping the same surface against the fence to make the finish cut. The wood seen here is western cedar from a local lumber yard, selected for its tight, uniform grain pattern. The exact same technique is used for making guitar backs from solid hardwoods like walnut, cherry, and maple.

Assemble the Panel

Before gluing your top or back panel, check to make sure the edges align with no gaps. If gaps are visible between the two pieces, use a plane or jointer to smooth them and make them fit perfectly to each other.

To glue, put bar clamps on a flat surface and apply a bead of glue along the edge of one piece of stock **(N).**Tighten the bar clamps slowly to press the two stock pieces together, creating a panel with symmetry of grain pattern and color **(O)**. Leave the clamps in place for hours before the next steps. You may need a weight to keep the panel flat.

Scrape away the excess glue. If you have access to a drum sander, use it to bring the resawn panel to a uniform thickness. Without one, use a hand plane to smooth the joint where the two pieces are glued **(P)**.

Complete the Panels

Before the top panel is ready, two things are required. The sound hole must be drilled and strips added to strengthen the seam in the panel. Place the box body over the top to plan the placement of the sound hole; adjust a circle cutter to drill an appropriately sized hole. Pencil it in place; the center of the hole should correspond with the centerline between the two pieces of the top **(Q)**. Use the circle cutter to drill until the center drill pokes through and then turn the stock over to drill from the other side **(R)**. By drilling

Leave the glued panel in the clamps until the glue sets. If the panel lifts slightly under clamping pressure, place weights on top.

A drum sander is the perfect way to smooth both sides of the glued panel. Scrape away excess glue first with either a scraper or block plane.

Mark the sound hole location on the underside of the top panel, using the box sides to help frame its location.

Drill the sound hole partly through from one side. Turn it over. The center hole shows where to lower the drill for finishing.

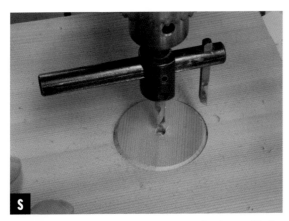

By drilling in from both sides, a clean-edged sound hole is formed.

Add thin strips of wood to the underside of the top to strengthen the seam.

Glue and clamp the strips in place to strengthen the seam of the back panel.

halfway through from both sides, the cleanest possible hole is formed, requiring the least sanding **(S).** Note that the back panel does not have a sound hole.

With the box sides temporarily in place on the top, measure and cut thin strips of wood to strengthen the seam on both sides of the hole **(T).** Cut the pieces about ⅛-inch (3mm) shy of the sound hole so they will not be visible at the edge in the finished guitar. Spread glue on the underside of the strips and use clamps to hold them securely to the underside of the guitar top. Similar strips should be planned to fit the seam on the guitar back **(U).**

The final step in preparing the top is to put a strip on the underside to help support the bridge **(V).** To determine the location for this strip, you must know the distance between the nut and bridge. This is most critical if making a fretted guitar. When the glue has dried, follow the steps for attaching the top and back on page 67.

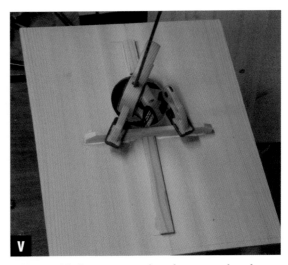

Add cross blocking to strengthen the area under where the bridge will mount.

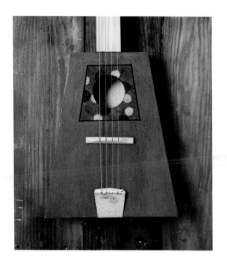

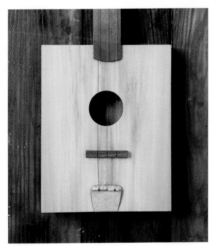

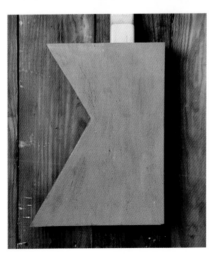

Chapter 6

FINISHING

A box guitar in which you've made the box from scratch is a clear invitation to finish and decorate exactly as you choose. You can choose to paint it, leave it unpainted, or if you've used beautiful woods, you can use a clear finish. When I taught my students at the Clear Spring School how to build their own guitars, they used a variety of creative techniques in decorating theirs; a simple guitar box can serve as a palette for designs sourced in your own imaginations. Personally, I am not the painterly type, and look for simple means when finishing my guitars. This chapter is intended to simply make some suggestions to get your own creative juices flowing.

TOOLS & MATERIALS

Your choice of the following:	Powdered milk paint	Brushes
Clear Danish oil	Acrylic paint	Lint-free cloth
Water-based polyurethane	Permanent marker	Masking tape
	Woodburner	Pouncer

CLEAR DANISH OIL

If you love the colors of real wood, a clear Danish oil finish reveals the beauty of grain and allows the natural colors to shine through. A bit of warning, however. Clear finishes accentuate any coarse sanding marks and spots of unnecessary glue adhered in places where you may not want to see them in your finished guitar. Pay particular attention to sanding prior to application of clear finishes, if you are wanting to use your box guitar as an example of your careful craftsmanship. To apply Danish oil, brush it on, then wipe it off **(A)**. Apply two or three coats **(B)**.

CONTRASTING NECK AND BODY

Another idea is to use a clear finish on the neck and then paint the body a contrasting color. Remember to remove the sanding marks from the neck first, unless you are aiming for a truly rustic look. Water-based polyurethane in a satin sheen is a good choice for finishing a guitar neck **(C)**. After the finish has thoroughly dried, apply masking tape to keep paint from getting on the neck **(D)**.

Use a clear Danish oil finish to bring out the beauty of the wood. Brush it on to get adequate penetration, and then wipe dry.

The entire guitar, one end to the other, is now protected by a clear finish.

To finish the neck, brush on water-based polyurethane.

Use masking tape to prevent paint from getting on the neck.

Add water to powdered milk paint until it has a cream-like consistency.

Apply the milk paint with a brush.

Milk paint is an interesting choice for the box. When layered with one color under another, a light sanding reveals a blending of colors that makes the guitar box look worn by decades of use. It is also easy to use. Simply mix a tablespoon or two of dry milk paint power with enough water to turn it to the consistency of cream **(E)**. Brush it on and let it dry **(F)**. Apply additional layers of the same or different colors, lightly sanding between coats. When the last layer of paint is dry, do a bit of heavier sanding. You now have a lovely smooth surface for whatever additional embellishment you choose next.

SPLATTER TECHNIQUE

Another favorite decorative method is Jackson Pollock's technique of splattering paint. It is risky, in that the results are somewhat unpredictable. A bit of practice on cardboard is good preparation before you attack your lovely guitar box with paint. The paint is shaken from the brush by a quick flick of the wrist. Only through some practice will you know how much to put on the brush. You will want to do your splattering outside and in old clothes, as it can be messy. Mask off the neck with masking tape before you attach the body of the guitar unless you want to paint it, too. Select a few different colors and apply one layer at a time; allow each layer to dry before applying the next **(G, H,** and **I)**. Knowing when to stop is the most important consideration. When you get a look you are pleased with, use clear water-based polyurethane finish to protect the lovely paint job **(J)**. If you aren't pleased with the splattering, you can sand and start over before applying the clear finish.

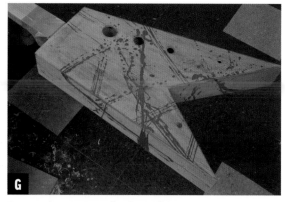

Begin splattering on the first color.

Allow the first color to dry fully before the next is applied.

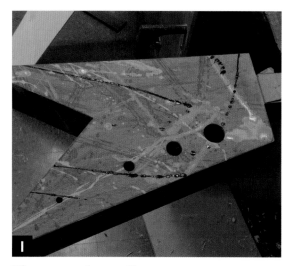

When you get what you like, stop.

Apply water based polyurethane to deepen the color and protect the milkpaint from wear.

Choose an acrylic paint and apply a solid color base coat first, and then use masking tape to mark areas for accent colors.

After the first accent color has dried, apply a second round of masking tape. On the guitar pictured, a red outline is being made around the yellow triangle.

After painting, the fretboard can be glued in place, and the whole guitar finished in clear water-based polyurethane.

ACRYLIC PAINT

Acrylic paint from your local craft supply store is available in many colors and is also useful for finishing and decorating your box guitar. Unlike milk paint, acrylic does not sand and blend as easily between coats, but instead offers a stronger color contrast. In some cases (like the guitar pictured), you may want to add a separate fretboard that lays over the body of the guitar. In such cases, mask off the neck while the body is being finished. Brush on the base coat, and then after it has dried, have fun with the addition of other colors. Use masking tape as a stencil to highlight areas and create shapes (**K**). Use additional masking tape to continue forming the design around the sound hole (**L**). Finally, glue the fretboard in place after the painting and decoration is complete (**M**). Apply a clear water-based finish.

POUNCER

A foam pouncer is a great way to apply paint without the use of a brush, and the round paint marks can be useful in creating a consistent design. In the guitar shown, an area was masked off and a pouncer used to apply acrylic paint over milk paint (**N**).

Use pouncers to apply a base coat to a color zone defined by masking tape.

Use pouncers of different sizes and with different colors to build on the pattern. Random is good **(O)**. Use a permanent marker to outline the design area for additional interest and emphasis after the masking tape has been removed **(P)**. Use a straightedge or ruler as a guide to mark the line. After the design is complete, use a clear water-based polyurethane finish to protect the beauty of your guitar box **(Q)**. Another option is to use the pouncers to make a ring around a round sound hole. Adding polka dots can be a great way to make a clown guitar **(R)**.

WOODBURNING

If you have a plain wooden box, like the ones used in a kit guitar, another option is to use a woodburner to create a pattern **(S)**. Think of your guitar box as an empty canvas with which you can experiment and have fun!

Apply additional colors after the base coat has dried.

Peel away the masking tape and use a permanent marker to create a strong border line around your design.

Apply a protective coat of water-based polyurethane finish.

Use pouncers of various sizes to make polka dots. Use masking tape to cover the portion of the box where the neck is to be attached.

Use a woodburning pen to create a pattern on your box. Even with minimal drawing skills, interesting patterns can be made.

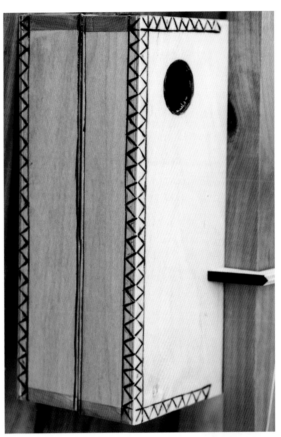

A simple hammered tailpiece gives a secure attachment for strings, and is easy to make from common sheet metal.

TAILPIECES

Tailpieces are one of the fun parts of making a guitar. All kinds of design opportunities are present in this simple part.

Make a Sheet Metal Tailpiece

Common sheet metal is a simple way to create a tailpiece (M). In combination with metal stamps, a sheet metal tailpiece provides a spot to name the guitar.

Create the Tailpiece

Use a fine-tip permanent marker to design your tailpiece directly on the sheet metal and then cut along the lines you've drawn with common metal-cutting snips (N). Use a sanding block or belt sander to smooth the final shape (O). Round the edges so that there will be no sharp points to interfere with your enjoyment of your finished guitar (P).

Use metal-cutting shears to cut a piece to size. One end wider than the other is a pleasing shape.

Use a stationary belt sander to sand the edges smooth and round the corners.

Rounded corners help to avoid sharp edges and create a more finished look.

Customize the Tailpiece

The round end of a ball-peen hammer creates a nice texture (**Q**). Use a center punch to mark the locations for holes in your tailpiece. Photo **R** shows the completed punching for four strings, and screw holes to attach the tailpiece to the guitar in progress. Drill the holes.

Letter stamps are the perfect way to personalize your guitar or name it. An anvil is helpful, as well as a ball-peen hammer. Be careful in the placement of letters, as it is common to place letters backward by mistake (**S**).

Shape the Tailpiece

To fit over the end of the guitar, an almost 90° bend is required in the tailpiece. Place one end in the vise and use your thumbs to press the other end into the desired shape. A bit of hammering while the tailpiece is still in the vise may be required (**T**).

Use a ball-peen hammer and anvil to make the tailpiece look old and distressed.

Measure and mark the locations for strings and for screw holes for mounting. A center punch helps the drill to penetrate the metal without going off course.

Use letter stamps to name your guitar or sign it.

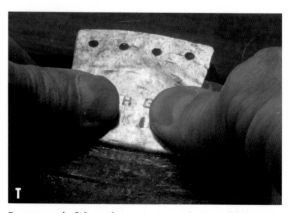

Put one end of the tailpiece in a metal vise to fold it over for mounting to your guitar.

Put a gentle bend in the other end of the tailpiece to provide clearance for the strings to pass through the holes and across the top of the guitar.

Carefully align the tailpiece to the neck, nut, and planned location for the bridge. Then mark for screws.

To bring the tailpiece to its final shape, make a slight bend in a line along the string holes. This is required to allow the strings to pass through and to make room for the ends of the steel strings **(U)**.

Install the Tailpiece

To install your tailpiece, careful alignment is required so the strings will be held uniformly along the neck. Use a straightedge to help position the tailpiece as you mark the screw holes **(V)**. The finished steel tailpiece, secured with screws, provides a robust attachment for strings **(W** and **X)**.

Install pan-head screws to hold the tailpiece in place.

The hand-crafted metal tailpiece is an effective way to attach strings, but also a great way to personalize your work.

Make a Hinge Tailpiece

You can use a hinge to attach the strings, but sometimes the hinge holes are too large to capture the end of the string. Use brass grommets like those used in the tail end of a kit guitar to reduce the diameter of the hole in brass hinges **(Y).** Slip the grommet through the hole and use a punch to flare it out on the opposite side **(Z).** The finished hinge has holes small enough that the end of the steel strings will not pass through **(AA).** Mount the hinge so that the barrel of the hinge rests its 90° bend where the top and end of the guitar are joined. The screws that came with the hinge can be used to secure it in place.

Make a Clear Acrylic Tailpiece

You may want to use other materials to make a tailpiece for your guitar. For the Jackson Pollock–inspired scissor-tailed guitar, it was undesirable for the tailpiece to interfere visually with the painting on the top. A clear acrylic sheeting tailpiece and bridge were the perfect solution. Designing a tailpiece to fit such an oddly shaped guitar presented a challenge that may also be faced by you, dear reader, in the event you wish to make such a thing.

Another popular way to attach strings is to use a hinge, with one end attached to the body of the guitar and the other holding one end of each string. If the holes in the hinge are too large, small grommets work great.

Place one grommet in each hole on the string side and hammer with a punch.

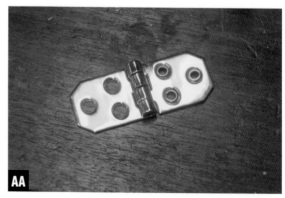

With the grommets in place, the hinge holes are reduced in size so that the end of the string will not pass through.

Other materials can also be used to attach strings. Use a straightedge to carefully calculate the intended position first. Use masking tape to avoid marking directly on the front of your guitar.

Transfer your marks directly onto the tailpiece stock.

Use a drill press to make the holes for the strings and screws to pass through.

Mark the String Positions

The first step is simply to determine the position of the strings to make certain they will travel across the bridge and up the length of the neck with the right position and spacing for ease of play. Apply painter's masking tape to the top of the guitar and carefully mark the position of each string; use that information to plan the tailpiece **(BB)**.

Cut the Material

Next, cut a piece of acrylic to the necessary size with a compound mitersaw or a very fine blade in a scroll saw, allowing extra material at each side and enough width so that it can be screwed to the end of the guitar. Hold the tailpiece in position while you mark the location of each string **(CC)**.

Drill and Sand the Tailpiece

Drill the holes for both the strings and screw holes for mounting the tailpiece to the end of the guitar **(DD)**. Sand the edges smooth. Working with acrylic sheeting requires very fine sanding if you want to make the edges clear. So after sanding with sandpaper up to 400 grit, polish the edges on a polishing wheel with fine abrasive. Then use screws to attach the tailpiece to the end of the guitar.

MAKE A KIT-STYLE TAILPIECE

The tailpiece for a kit guitar is built into the neck and is simply
formed by holes drilled through and reinforced by brass grommets.

1

Mark and drill.
Carefully mark the location for the holes and then drill
all the way through with a ⅛-inch (3mm) drill bit.

2

Continue drilling.
Use backing under the neck as you drill to prevent
tearout.

3

Sand the neck.
Before installing the brass grommets, sand the end of
the neck round and smooth to the touch.

4

Add the grommets.
Tap the grommets into place from each side of the neck.

Chapter 8

BRIDGES and NUTS

The bridge and the nut on a guitar control the height of the strings above the body and neck of the guitar. Bridges and nuts can be made in a variety of ways. The easiest bridge to make is little more than a piece of wood that rises above the top of the guitar and either rests upon it, held in place by the tension from the strings, or can be glued in place when its position must be of absolute certainty as it is with a fretted guitar. A more complicated design is a ukulele-style bridge you can find on page 127. A nut can be as simple as a 5⁄16-inch (8mm) diameter threaded rod, as seen in the kit guitar on page 18, or a 5⁄16- by 1½-inch (8 by 38mm) set screw. Be sure to reference the illustrations on page 163.

THE PURPOSE OF THE BRIDGE AND NUT

The placement of the bridge on the body of the guitar controls the length of the strings. When the neck is fretted, the distance between nut and bridge becomes critical. The distance between frets is related to the overall string length determined by the placement of the bridge and nut.

In an electric guitar, bridges are an excellent means to house and hide the piezo that transfers the vibrations of the strings into an electric impulse and then to the amp. Hiding the piezo in the bridge will be covered in the chapter on electrifying your guitar (page 105).

TOOLS & MATERIALS

Hardwood of choice	Compound miter saw, hand saw, or tablesaw with sled	Stop block	Belt sander or sanding block	Glue
Plane		Pencil	Drill press and bits of choice	Clamps
Tablesaw		Square		Fret saw
				File

FRETLESS GUITARS

Some of the concerns about nut and bridge placement are alleviated in a fretless box guitar because the slide being in contact with the strings is what shortens the length of the strings to change pitch. The exact distance between neck and strings is not a big concern on a non-fretted guitar. So in that case, simply having sufficient space between the neck and the strings is consideration enough. For that reason, it is actually much easier to make an unfretted guitar. But that's a good thing: you can start with the very basics to make a guitar that you can play and build greater complication into your next guitars as your skill develops.

MAKE A BRIDGE AND NUT

To make your own wooden bridge and nut, use hardwoods. Persimmon is the only North American member of the ebony family, so it is known for being dense and hard. One of the advantages of persimmon over real ebony is that persimmon grows all over the southeastern United States, while ebony is a protected and very expensive species. Other particularly dense hardwoods, like maple and black locust, are also acceptable choices. Whether you are making a bridge and nut from hardwood or some other material like clear acrylic sheeting, the steps will be the same.

A

Use the tablesaw to prepare stock for making bridges and nuts. Tilt the blade 15° to make stock from which a number of bridges or nuts can be formed.

B

Use a compound miter saw, tablesaw with sled, or hand saw to cut bridges and nuts to length. If making multiples, a stop block clamped to the fence of the saw will assure that each is the same length.

Cut the Stock

Both the bridge stock and nut stock start at the same point. Plane your bridge and nut stock down to a uniform thickness (about ¼-inch [6mm]), and make a 45° angle cut on the tablesaw to determine its shape **(A)**. You will find that it is much safer and easier to work material about 15 to 18 inches (38 to 46cm) long rather than to shape

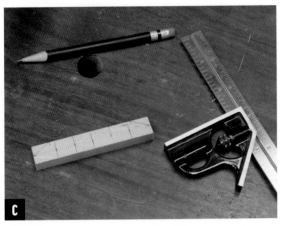

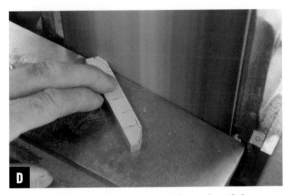

Carefully mark the position of decorative holes (if you choose to use them), and the shape you intend, as well as the string positions.

Sand the bridge to shape using a belt sander. If choosing a hand tool approach, simply saw the shape and sand with a sanding block.

You can use other materials like clear acrylic, but in each case the process is the same, and sanding is required.

short pieces to make a bridge or nut, so plan to make several at once for your next guitars rather than just one. Use the compound miter saw with stop block, a hand saw, or a sled on the tablesaw with stop block to cut the bridge and nut pieces to length. Regardless of tool choice, a stop block is required if you are making uniform parts for more than one guitar **(B)**.

Shape the Parts

Carefully measure and mark the locations for grooves for strings and other decorative features; the bridge is shown here **(C)**. Sand it to shape **(D and E)**. Similar steps are taken in the early stages of making the nut. Holes can be drilled in bridges to lighten them and help communicate vibration into the top of the guitar **(F)**.

Use the drill press to drill decorative holes in your bridge, if you choose.

ABOUT THE GROOVES

Grooves cut in these two parts control the spacing between strings. If the bridge and nut are too low or if the grooves are cut too deep, the strings will buzz on the frets of a fretted guitar. If the bridge and nut are too high, it takes more finger pressure to change the note, and pressing down too great a distance stretches the string and changes the pitch. Finding just the right balance in height of strings over the neck is a matter of careful judgment and some fine tuning.

Use a small fret saw to cut the locations for the strings to fit the bridge and nut. The spacing should be carefully planned. Widen the cut where needed to allow for the thickness of each string.

Cut the Grooves

In forming either the bridge or nut, grooves to hold the strings in position must be cut. This operation can be performed after the bridge or nut are glued in place on the neck and body of the guitar, or while the parts are held securely in a vise. Cutting while the parts are held in the vice is the preferred method as it allows you to start over with a new part if you make a mistake. Cut the grooves with a fret saw (**G** and **H**). Finally, use a fine-tooth file to widen the grooves to fit the strings (**I**). If desired, attach the nut and bridge to the guitar with glue (recommended for fretted guitars).

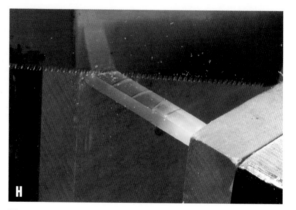

Use a saw to cut grooves in the clear acrylic.

Widen the groove for the strings with a thin file.

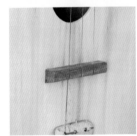

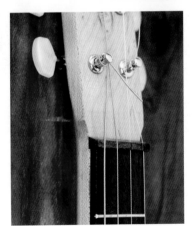

Chapter 9

ELECTRIFYING
Your GUITAR

There are at least three ways to turn your box guitar electric so that it can be plugged into an amp or a computer (to record and edit your play). One simple way is to use a clip-on piezo that can be clipped in place to the sound hole, and then removed when not in use. Another slightly more complicated means is to glue disc piezos to the underside of the guitar top during the assembly process. A slight improvement over that approach is the use of a bar-type piezo embedded in the bridge. The advantage of the embedded bar-type piezo is that it receives its vibrations more strongly and directly from the strings. The disadvantage is that wiring either of these permanently attached electronic pickup systems require that you plan early in the box making process, or at least before the top and back are permanently glued in place. Be sure to reference the illustration on page 164.

TOOLS & MATERIALS

Piezo, either a bar or disc type	Wire	Drill or drill press and ¼- and ⅜-inch (6 and 10mm) bits	Sanding block or hand plane	Screwdriver
Volume control pot	Wire stripper	Chisel	Painter's tape	Rasp
¼-inch (6mm) amp cord connector jack	Soldering iron	Pencil	Glue	Router table with ⅛-inch (3mm) straight-cut router bit
Volume knob	Solder	Bandsaw	Clamps	
	Flux		Screws	

INSTALL A SIMPLE PIEZO KIT

The easiest way to electrify your guitar is to use a kit. For example, C.B. Gitty offers prewired no-solder kits for wiring a box guitar **(A).** To install this type of kit, simply leave an access port as described on page 108 and use the lock nuts to hold the parts in place. The piezo is glued to the underside of the top near the bridge using the self-adhesive tape.

INSTALL A SOLDERED PIEZO KIT

To wire a guitar, you will need some simple parts that can be acquired either as a wiring kit or as separate parts in larger quantities. In photo **B,** clockwise from left, the parts are: a bar-type piezo made for four strings; a volume control potentiometer (or "pot" for short); a ¼-inch (6mm) amp cord connector jack; and a "chicken head" volume knob.

Make the Solder Joints

There are excellent internet videos and tutorials on how to solder and it is a skill that requires practice. With only minimum soldering skills and a simple schematic that applies to both disc and bar piezos (page 164), you can make your own wiring harness in no time.

Lay your parts out carefully in an arrangement as you see exactly in the schematic and leave extra wire between parts to ease putting them in place on the inside of your guitar. Use a soldering iron and resin core solder to securely attach the wires **(C).**

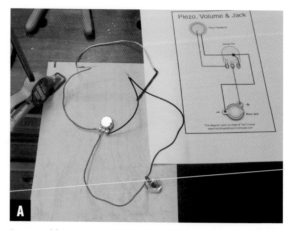

Prewired kits are available that eliminate the necessity of developing soldering skills.

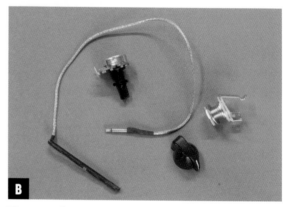

These are the parts required: a piezo (either a bar or disc type), a volume pot, a ¼-inch jack, and a control knob.

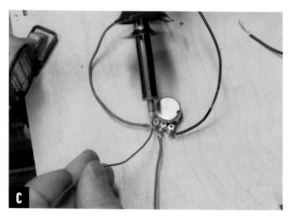

To solder, carefully lay out your parts to fit the schematic, strip the wires, and bend them over as shown to prepare for solder. If soldering for the first time, practice first.

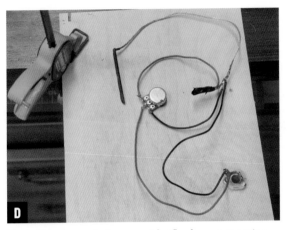

Your soldering technique must be flawless, so practice first and make sure that your soldered joints are secure.

Drill a ¼-inch hole for your volume control knob, if you choose to use one.

A ⅜-inch hole is required for the ¼-inch jack that fits the amp cord. Drill it in a spot where the cord will not interfere with your play.

It is best to wire and solder all these parts together prior to installation in your guitar, so do not be overly skimpy on the length of your wires. On a bar-type piezo, clip the connector plug from the wire first. Then, after stripping the inside wire, solder the red wire to it. After that connection is securely made, solder the black wires to the outer sheath **(D)**.

Modify the Guitar Body

There are two things that must be done before the back is added. First, drill a hole for the volume pot if you intend to be able to control the sound level at your guitar without having to walk over to the amp. You will need a ¼-inch (6mm) drill bit and to decide where the control would be most convenient. Consider a place toward the lower end of the guitar where it would be out of the way during play, but conveniently located without reaching too far **(E)**.

You will likely also want the ¼-inch (6mm) wiring jack to be mounted out of the way at the end of the guitar, but not on the front. First, drill a hole in the location desired for the jack to fit **(F)**.

If necessary, chisel on the inside to thin the area where the jack will pass through the stock, or buy an extended jack of greater length **(G).** If you are thoughtful in designing your guitar, you can drill a larger hole from the inside of the stock prior to assembly for the larger portion of the jack to nest.

Modify the Back Panel

If using electronic parts in a guitar, there is always the possibility of failure or that you've failed to get it wired right in the first place. In either case, you will want some way to get into the inside of the guitar to get things right, and the sound hole will not be large enough to do whatever fixing or replacement of parts may be required. Fortunately, it is rather easy to provide access through a hole in the back, and without affecting the sound. Let's design the back of the box so that it can be opened and so that the electrical components can be added.

Plan the back of the guitar so that a section can be screwed off **(H).** Then use the bandsaw to make the necessary cut, and sand or plane the edge perfectly flat. Lay the back in place on the guitar sides with another piece of Baltic birch plywood laid underneath. Trace a line where this piece can be cut **(I).**

Sometimes the cord jack placement will require chiseling a flat spot on the inside so that the jack would fit through the thicker stock.

With the back laid temporarily in place, draw where you want your access hatch to fit. It must allow for you to easily service or replace parts.

Trace a line on additional stock so that you can make an access hatch that will fit tightly.

Tape the access hatch stock to the back panel of your guitar.

Lay the guitar on its back to trace the shape of the hatch.

Use the bandsaw to cut the access hatch to the correct size and shape. Make your cuts just outside the line so the back can be smoothed to the sides of the guitar after it is put in place.

After cutting that line and making certain the line is planed or sanded flat, tape the two pieces together **(J)**. Position the guitar box upside down with the edges of the back aligned to the sides. You can now trace the outlines of the hatch **(K)**. With the shape marked on the Baltic birch plywood, remove the tape and use the bandsaw to cut the hatch door to shape **(L)**.

Attach the Back and Hatch

Once the shape of the hatch is cut (leaving some extra stock at the edge to be smoothed after assembly) glue the back in place **(M)**.

Glue the back panel on, using plenty of clamps.

When the glue has set, use screws to attach the hatch door. You could countersink the screw holes so they will be flush, or (depending on the design of your guitar) you could choose to use pan head or round head screws for a more rustic look **(N).** After the back panel and access hatch are firmly in place, use a plane, rasps, and sanding blocks to smooth the edges in preparation for your next steps.

INSTALL A BAR PIEZO IN A BRIDGE

Certainly, the easiest way to electrify a guitar is by using a clip-on piezo or by using a piezo glued or taped to the underside of the top. A bar-type piezo offers the advantage of being more directly in contact with the vibrations from each string, and can be mounted in a space routed for it in the bridge. This can be most easily and accurately be accomplished through the use of a ⅛-inch (3mm) straight-cut router bit mounted in the router table and raised to cut a height equal to that of the thickness of the bar piezo. Set up stops to control the travel of the stock so that the router cut does not extend past the ends of the bridge **(O).** The bridge perfectly milled for the piezo to fit should hold the piezo at the center and with the bottom edge flush to the guitar's top **(P).** Installing a bridge-mounted piezo on the top of a guitar requires careful measuring if the instrument has frets, as the distance between the bridge and the nut is crucial for the proper intonation of a fretted instrument.

Use ½-inch-long wood screws to attach the access hatch.

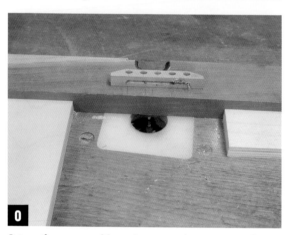

Set up the router table and stops as shown to rout the underside of a bridge for a bar-type piezo to fit.

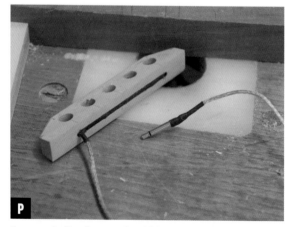

A properly fitted piezo should be centered end for end in the bridge and be flush on the underside.

Chapter 10

MAKE *a* UKULELE

If you have mastered some of the skills from making other box guitars in this book, you may want to try your hand at making this step-by-step ukulele. Ukes require less in the way of materials than a full-bodied guitar, and some of the process is made much easier by the inexpensive ready-made fretboards that are available from luthier suppliers and online. You'll notice that there are many steps involved with this project, but it's worth delving into. Be sure to reference the illustrations on page 165.

TOOLS & MATERIALS

Elm boards	Router table with ³⁄₁₆-inch (5mm)-radius roundover bit, flush-cutting bit, ½-inch (13mm) spiral straight-cut bit, and ⅛-inch (3mm) straight bit	Hardwood for back and top	Adjustable circle cutter	Parts to electrify uke (optional, see page 105)
Tablesaw		Bar clamps	Wood strips for top and back support	Utility knife
Belt sander or sanding block		Drum sander		Clear water-based polyurethane finish
Shaker-style boiling tank and hot plate		Hardwood for neck	Ratchet wrench with screwdriver bit	
Bending jig (page 165)	Glue	Coarse rasp	Wood strips for bridge	Brush
Clamps	Lining stock (purchased or made, see page 114)	Fine rasp	Router jig for bridge (page 166)	Tuners
Scrap wood		Sandpaper		Awl
Compound miter saw	Clothespins	Double-sided tape	⅛-inch (3mm) brass grommets	Wood for nut
Painter's tape	Self-adhesive sandpaper on a flat board	Drill press with ¹⁄₁₆- and ⅛-inch (2 and 3mm) bits		Fret saw
				File

BEND THE SIDES

This technique for making the bent sides for ukulele is a bit unusual in that it's derived from making bent wood boxes. Immersing thin wood in boiling water makes it soft and flexible to bend; when held to a form while it dries, the shape is retained. You can use this technique to make all kinds of curved shapes, including guitar bodies, but should expect it to be less precise than other methods. It is, however, no less fun.

Prepare the Jig

First, you will need to make a form upon which to bend your ukulele sides. It is useful to make the form so that it can be held in the vise on the work bench in a vertical manner, which gives a better view of whether you're bending both sides to be symmetrical. This jig can also be clamped to the workbench without a vise, but you will have to step back and observe from the side to see that your bending of sides is symmetrical. Follow the measurements in the drawing (page 165) to make your jig and assemble it with screws.

Prepare the Stock

Saw and sand the elm to a thickness of a bit less than ⅛-inch (3mm). Being cut this thin will allow the sides to bend after being boiled for about 10

A

Boil the ukulele sides in water to soften them for bending.

B

While the sides are hot and wet, clamp them in a bending form to hold them in shape as they cool and dry.

C

Clamp the ends so they overlap at each end of the bending form.

to 15 minutes or so. In preparing stock, watch for knots and other defects that might cause the wood to break during the bending process. Use a Shaker-style boiling tank and hot plate to boil both sides of the ukulele at the same time so they can both be quickly mounted on the bending jig (**A**).

Clamp the Sides to the Jig

Use clamps to hold the ends of the sides to the bending jig and use padding blocks to keep the clamps from marring the surface of the wood. Be careful to overlap the sides the same amount at each end so that when they are cut to length, they will be matched on each side (**B**). Use clamps to pull the sides in toward the center on both sides to give your instrument that classic ukulele shape (**C**). Place the clamping pressure equally on both sides toward the top of the instrument, allowing it to bulge larger at the bottom. Let the sides cool and dry thoroughly before removing them from the bending jig.

CUT THE SIDES

Use the compound miter saw or tablesaw to cut the joint where the two sides will meet, at both the top and bottom of the body of the uke. Tape the parts together, then place the centerline of the cut in alignment with the blade's path. A board held down on one side allows control of the cut without having your hands close to the blade **(D)**.

ATTACH THE SIDES

After the top and bottom cuts are made, use blocks of wood to join the two sides into a uniform shape. Add a touch of interior craftsmanship by routing the edges of your blocks used to join the sides **(E)**. Spread glue on the joining blocks so that they will be ready to clamp in place **(F)**. Use padding blocks to prevent marking of the outside of your uke as you clamp the sides together onto the interior blocks **(G)**.

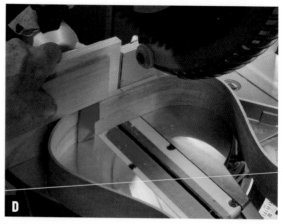

Mark the centerline where the two sides come together and carefully align them at that point. Use a compound miter saw or tablesaw to make the cut.

Use a ³⁄₁₆-inch-radius roundover bit in the router table to prepare glue blocks for joining the sides. Use a push block to control the workpiece through the operation to keep your fingers safe.

The side assembly of your uke will consist of four parts: a glue block at each end and the sides themselves.

Carefully align the ends as you glue the sides in place with the glue block at each end.

H

The finished assembly of sides will hold its shape for the next steps.

I

Use the tablesaw to make lining that is used to attach the sides to the top and back of the guitar. Rip thin strips from stock planed to the desired thickness.

After gluing and later removing the clamps, you will have given shape to the body of a uke **(H)**.

MAKE THE LINING STOCK

The next step is to make the lining stock. Lining stock can be purchased through your luthier supplier or made by following the steps shown here. Lining consists of flexible strips of wood that, when glued at the intersections of the top, sides, and back, add additional gluing surface and strength. Cuts made almost all the way through lining stock make it flexible enough to conform to the inside of a uke and follow its curves.

Prepare the Stock

To prepare for cutting lining stock, plane the wood to a thickness of 1 inch (25mm). Rip it into thin strips of about ¼-inch wide by ⁷⁄₁₆-inch high (6 by 11mm) **(I)**. Two pieces of lining will be ripped from each strip. To make lining stock more consistent with the kinds you can buy and to make the interior of the uke more craftsmanlike, make an angle cut on the edge at each side as shown **(J)**. Rip each strip into two pieces of lining material **(K)**.

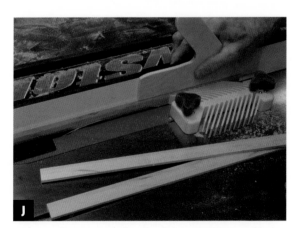

J

Make angle cuts on each side of the sawn pieces of lining stock. This thins the lining stock on the inside edge.

K

Use the tablesaw to cut the lining stock down the middle, forming two pieces from each strip.

Saw the Kerfs

Use the bandsaw to make cuts into the lining stock to an exact depth, and with each cut ³⁄₁₆-inch (5mm) apart. This may take some trial and error to get just right, as some woods will need to be cut deeper than others to achieve the necessary flexibility. These cuts can also be made with a fret saw, but you have to use great care to not cut too deep. A stop block mounted to the table of a bandsaw works well to control the depth **(L).** All these cuts can be tedious, but in just a few minutes you can make more than enough lining for attaching the top and bottom of a uke or two **(M).** The beveled side of the lining should face the saw blade, with the flat side being left uncut.

ATTACH THE LINING

Spread glue on the flat side of the lining and fit it to the inside of the body of the uke so that it is flush with the edge **(N).** Lining can be sawn or broken to fit in the space available. Clothespins make effective and inexpensive clamps to hold lining in place as the glue sets **(O).**

Use the bandsaw to make cuts along the face of each piece of lining stock. The blocking behind the blade controls the depth of each cut, and also assures that the cut does not go through.

Saw kerfs cut in the lining stock are what make it flexible enough to fit the curvature on the inside of the uke.

Apply glue to the lining as you bend it into place and apply clamps. Clothespins are a cheap means of applying necessary clamping pressure.

A bit of glue squeezed out from behind the lining is a good sign that you've applied enough.

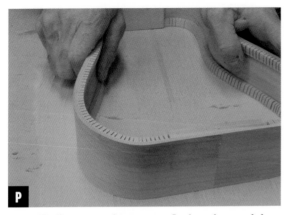

Use self-adhesive sandpaper on a flat board to sand the lining flush with the sides of the box. This will prevent any gaps when the top and bottom are glued in place.

Book-matching a back and top gives the most beautiful effect. Carefully tape the front side of the panel first so they are held tightly to each other.

After the glue has dried, sand the sides and linings flush on both sides to prepare for gluing the top and back in place. Self-adhesive sandpaper stuck to a flat board works well as a sanding surface. Simply move the sides back and forth with some force until the lining and sides are flush **(P)**.

MAKE A BACK AND TOP

Resaw a lovely hardwood for the back of your uke. A piece of cherry is shown here, book-matched so that the grain will be symmetrical. Tape the two pieces together **(Q)**. Fold the two pieces back and spread glue in the joint. This is the back side that will be inside the uke **(R)**. Use tape to pull the joint tight **(S)**. Use bar clamps to hold the two pieces in perfect alignment as the glue sets.

Fold the two pieces back on the hinge provided by the tape and spread glue in the joint.

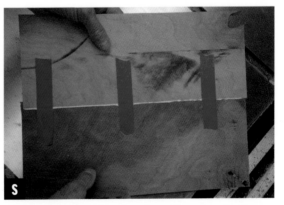

Tape the joint closed on the other side and apply clamps until the glue sets.

Use the same technique to make a top for your uke from western cedar or some other tone wood, and sand them to a finished thickness of about ⅛-inch (3mm) **(T)**. Use a drum sander to make certain these pieces are flat. If you want to electrify your uke, add any necessary holes and access hatches to the top and back at this point.

DESIGN THE NECK

Use the same technique for making ukulele necks that was used for making box guitar necks (page 39). This requires planing hardwood lumber to a thickness of ⅞-inch (22mm); ripping it to width; adding an additional block of hardwood to thicken the end where it attaches to the body of the instrument; and gluing an additional support block in place to assist when it comes time to guide it on the surface of the bandsaw. These steps are done following the instructions on page 39, but using the dimensions shown in the illustration (page 165). If using a commercially available fretboard as is shown here, trace it to help design the shape of the neck and the location of the peghead **(U)**.

Design the Peghead

When you have laid out the design on the top of the neck, it will be ready for your first steps at the bandsaw **(V)**.

After sanding, the beauty of the book-matched panel is revealed.

Lay a ukulele fretboard in place on the glued-up neck and design its shape. Sketching the shape of the peghead is also being shown.

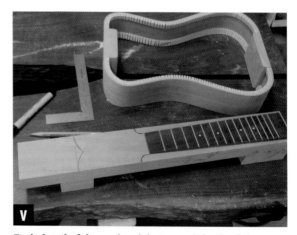

Each detail of the peghead design and the fit of the fretboard should be clearly marked for cutting.

Turn the neck on the side to plan the shape on the underside.

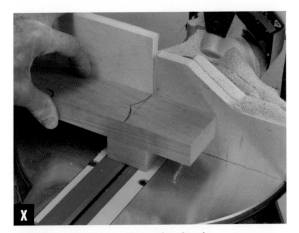

Trim the neck stock on the peghead end.

Continue your design work on the side of the uke neck, marking the shape of the peghead on the side. It must be angled as shown to allow the tuners to be lower in elevation than the nut and fretboard (**W**).

Shape the Peghead

Use the compound miter saw to trim the peghead end of the neck to length (**X**). Note that some of the blocking on the underside is left to support the neck while using the bandsaw in the next step. Trim the sides and top of the neck (**Y**). Note that some of the stock at the base end has been left unsawn so that it can be used to support subsequent cuts. Next cut the angled face of the peghead (**Z**).

Begin cutting the neck to shape by making cuts on both sides along where the fretboard will fit.

Cut the angled face of the peghead next.

Use the fence to guide the saw cut forming the underside of the peghead **(AA).** This technique is exactly as was done in forming the back side of the pegheads in making a box guitar (chapter 3). Move the fence out of the way to make the final cut in forming the back side of the peghead **(BB).**

Shape the Neck Base

Use the bandsaw to form the shape of the neck where it fits the body of the ukulele, first forming the curve on the underside **(CC).** Make angle cuts to give it a more interesting shape, using the fence to guide the cuts **(DD** and **EE).** For these steps, add a longer fence extension to give support to the full length of the neck.

Use the fence on the bandsaw to guide your cut in forming the backside of the peghead.

Finish forming the back of the peghead by moving the fence away and making a curved cut.

Shape the underside of the neck where it will fit the body of the ukulele.

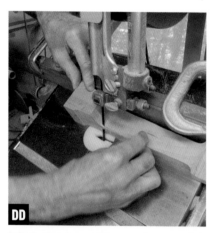

Tilt the bandsaw table to make an angled cut, further forming the underside of the neck where it fits the body of the uke. Cut in first with one side of the neck against the fence.

Finish the cut with the other side against the fence.

Use a coarse rasp to shape the neck, following lines you've carefully laid out on the underside.

Shape the Neck

Use a coarse rasp to begin shaping the neck so that it will be comfortable in your hands (**FF**). Continue with a fine rasp, sandpaper, and sanding blocks to make your finished neck (**GG, HH,** and **II**). To cut your neck to the finished length, use double-sided tape to secure it to the base of the compound miter saw. The tape will help to hold it square and secure as you cut away the end where it will need to attach squarely to the body of the uke (**JJ**).

Use a finer rasp as you get closer to completion.

Use sandpaper from coarse to fine to finish your neck.

Use small sanding blocks to finish the peghead end.

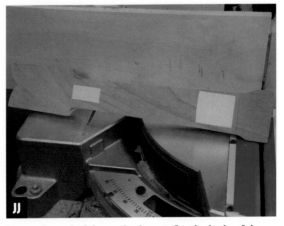

To cut the end of the neck where it fits the body of the uke, apply double-sided tape to the flat surface on top.

Line up the marking on the end with the line of the cut and make the cut **(KK)**.

CREATE THE SOUND HOLE

To determine the location of the sound hole, you will first want to locate the position of the bridge in relation to the fretboard and neck. Lay these out carefully and mark the centerpoint where the sound hole will be drilled **(LL)**. Use an adjustable circle cutter to form the hole **(MM)**. Drill partway through from one side and then the other to get the smoothest results and to avoid tearout. After the sound hole has been drilled, glue additional strips of wood in place to strengthen the seam where the top joins **(NN)**.

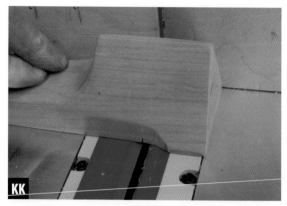

Adhere the neck to the top of the compound miter saw for this cut.

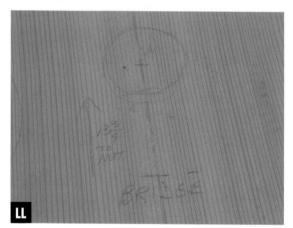

With the neck complete and cut to length, plan the location of the sound hole in the top of your uke. Note the location of the bridge marked in pencil.

Use a circle cutter in a drill press to drill partway through from one side, then the other.

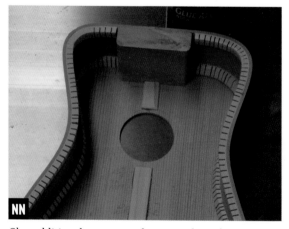

Glue additional support to the seam where the top is joined.

Clamp the pieces in place and wait until the glue sets.

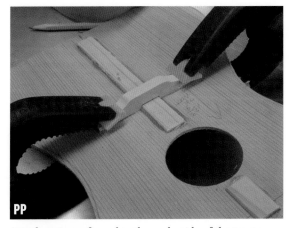

Attach a piece of wood to the underside of the top to support the bridge.

Use clamps to hold the top on tight as the glue sets.

Clamp these in place as the glue sets **(OO)**. Also add additional support under where the bridge will be glued to the top of the uke **(PP)**.

ATTACH THE TOP

To attach the top, spread glue on the lining and sides **(QQ)**. Use clamps to hold the top in position as the glue sets **(RR)**. Use a flush-cutting router bit to make the edges of the top even with the sides **(SS)**. This can also be done with a round sanding block, but the router makes it fast and accurate.

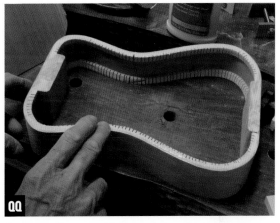

To prepare for assembly, spread glue along the lining and sides.

When the glue has dried, use a flush-cutting bit in the router table to trim the edges flush.

ATTACH THE NECK

Carefully mark the locations for pilot holes to attach the neck. The pilot holes must be sized only slightly smaller than the size of the screws used to avoid splitting the neck. Clamp the neck in a vertical position to drill the pilot hole, being careful that the depth of the hole is only slightly less than the length of the screw that will extend beyond the body of your uke **(TT).** Drill a matching hole in the block in the body of the uke. Use a ratchet wrench with screwdriver bit to tighten the screw that holds the neck to the body of the uke **(UU).** After one screw is put in position, a second screw hole is added to strengthen the attachment and prevent the neck from twisting in relation to the body of the uke. Make certain that the neck and the top of the uke are perfectly flush and tighten the screws.

ATTACH THE BACK

Spread glue on the lining and sides of the ukulele as you prepare to attach the back **(VV).** Then use clamps to hold the back in place as the glue dries **(WW).**

To prepare for attaching the neck, drill a pilot hole for a screw to fit.

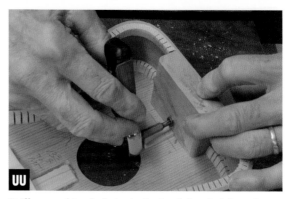

Drill a matching hole in the body of the ukulele and drive a screw through into the neck.

With the neck firmly connected and flush with the top, apply glue to the lining so that the back can be glued in place.

Clamp the back in place, and be careful to check the seams at all the edges to assure that they are tight.

XX

Spread glue on the back of the fretboard.

YY

Use clamps to hold the fretboard in place as the glue sets.

ZZ

Rip stock for your ukulele style bridge. This requires three steps, but working in long strips allows you to keep your hands safe, and multiples to be made at once.

ATTACH THE FRETBOARD

Spread glue on the underside of the fretboard as you prepare to glue it in place on the neck of your uke **(XX)**. With the fretboard carefully aligned on the neck, use clamps to hold it while the glue sets **(YY)**. Note the option shown here to shape the fretboard slightly at the lower end to harmonize (visually) with the shape of the sound hole.

CREATE THE BRIDGE

Shop-made ukulele bridges are a bit more complex than the bridges seen in chapter 8. The strings pass through the bridge instead of just over it, and it also serves as the anchor point for the strings because there isn't a tailpiece on a ukulele.

Cut the Stock

Plane and rip your stock to thickness and width, and then make a series of cuts partway through on the tablesaw. See the illustration on page 166 for more detail. Careful adjustment of fence position and blade height must be made. The blade should be set to cut $\frac{5}{32}$-inch (4mm) deep and the first cut should be made $\frac{5}{32}$-inch (4mm) from one edge of the stock. The second cut should be made $\frac{7}{16}$-inch (11mm) from the edge. A third cut is made at a 45° angle to allow the strings clearance to travel over the bridge (see **ZZ**). When the bridge stock is formed, use a tablesaw or compound miter saw to cut it to length. As in making a simpler bridge, it is far better and far safer to make enough stock for several rather than just one.

Shape the Ends

Shaping the flat ends of the bridge is a bit more complex and requires a router table, a special shop-made jig (see illustration on page 166), and a ½-inch (13mm) spiral straight-cut router bit **(AAA)**. Clamp the bridge to the jig and rotate it through the cut, first one end and then the other, with the jig being moved in a counter-clockwise manner.

Create the String Holes

Use the drill press to drill the holes for the strings to fit. Carefully mark the locations for the strings so that you have proper spacing between them. The holes will be on the underside furthest from the tablesaw cuts. The first bit is sized to fit the largest string that will pass through the hole, or about ¹⁄₁₆-inch (2mm). Follow that with a ⅛-inch (3mm) bit going only about ⅛-inch (3mm) into the wood **(BBB).** Insert brass grommets into the holes **(CCC).** An ⅛-inch (3mm)-thick piece of wood, plastic, ivory, or bone fits into the bridge to carry the strings and hold them at the right height over the body and neck. After the bridge is completed, you can modify its shape by using a scroll saw or other tools, particularly if you plan to use it with a tailpiece for the attachment of strings. Carefully sand the bridge.

After the ukulele bridges are cut to length, a special jig for the router table allows the shaping of the ends.

Drill holes for the strings to fit.

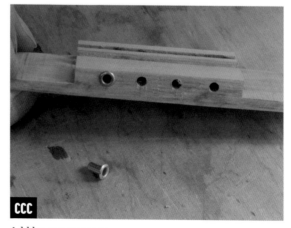

Add brass grommets.

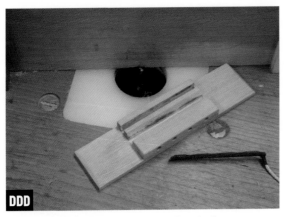

DDD

Use a ⅛-inch straight router bit so that the bar type piezo fits from the top, just under the part that supports the strings.

EEE

Align the router cut so that it fits in the saw kerf cut in the top of the bridge for the string support strip to fit. Move the bridge carefully between stops.

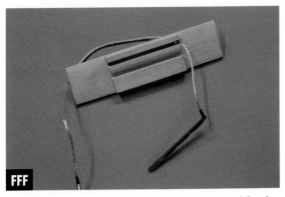

FFF

Drill a hole through the routed groove at one end for the wire to pass through.

ELECTRIFY THE UKE

Adding a bar-type piezo to a ukulele bridge is similar to the process with a normal bridge, but instead of routing on the underside of the bridge, set up the router so that the cut is inside the top saw kerf on the top of the bridge (**DDD**). When you have the router set up for this operation, place the bridge upside down on the router table and rout between stops (**EEE**). After routing, you will need to drill a hole at one end of the routed groove or the other so that the piezo's connecting wire can pass through (**FFF**).

PREPARE FOR FINISH

Sand the top, back, and sides. Apply tape to the top and mark the location of your bridge. The location must be precisely determined in order for the established distance between frets to give the correct tone (**GGG**).

GGG

Apply tape to the area where the bridge will fit so you can trace around it.

Cut carefully around the bridge so that its position, marked in tape, will shield the wood in that spot from the application of finish. This step will allow the bridge to be glued directly to the wood for greater strength **(HHH).**

APPLY THE FINISH

Apply a clear brush-on water-based polyurethane finish **(III).** Apply the finish to one area at a time to avoid drips and runs **(JJJ).** Then when the finish is complete, glue the bridge in place **(KKK).**

HHH

Cut carefully around the bridge and peel away the excess tape, leaving only the area in blue where the bridge will be attached.

III

Apply finish to your uke.

JJJ

The water-based polyurethane looks like milk as it is applied, but dries clear and offers protection to your uke.

KKK

Remove the masking tape on the top of the uke and use a clamp and glue to attach the bridge.

LLL

Mark the locations for the tuners.

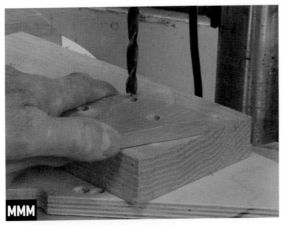

Use the drill press to drill the holes to fit your tuners.

Carefully predrill the holes for the screws to fit, holding your tuners in place.

Make a nut to fit at the top of the bridge. A small fret saw can be used to fit the strings.

INSTALL THE TUNERS

Carefully mark the locations for the tuners and use an awl to make a starting point for the drill **(LLL)**. Then use the drill press or hand-held electric drill to form the holes for the tuners to fit **(MMM)**. Drill pilot holes for the screws and install the tuners **(NNN)**.

COMPLETE THE UKE

Make a nut to hold the strings apart and at the necessary height using a fret saw **(OOO)**. Be sure to angle the cuts so the strings engage the nut as close as possible to the fretboard **(PPP)**. Widen the grooves slightly with a file to fit the various string sizes. Add strings and you're ready to play!

Angle your cut so that the strings engage the nut as close as possible to the fretboard side.

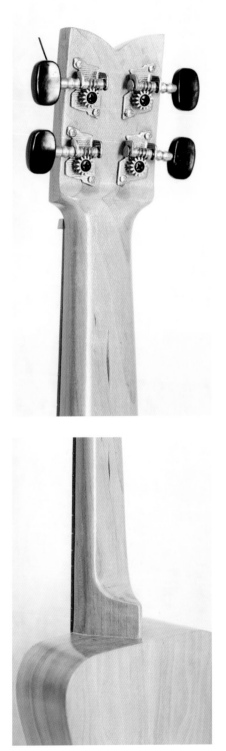

GALLERY OF FINISHED GUITARS

The mix and match photographs featured throughout the book at the ends of the chapters are close-ups of the following guitars built by Doug Stowe. Front, side, and back views are given for each. Note that for guitars where both sides are similar, only one side is shown.

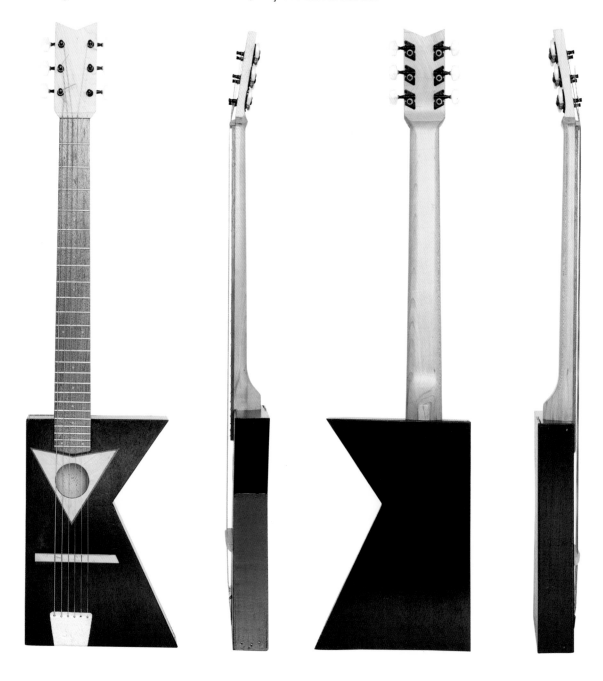

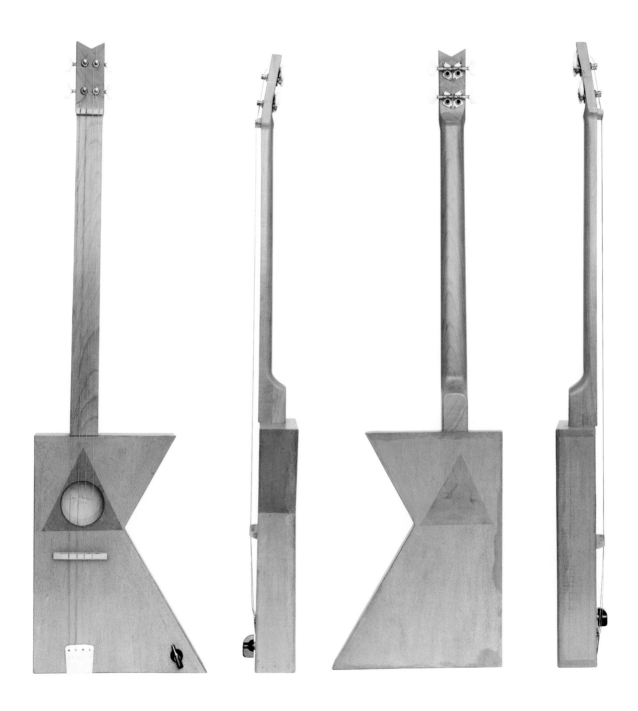

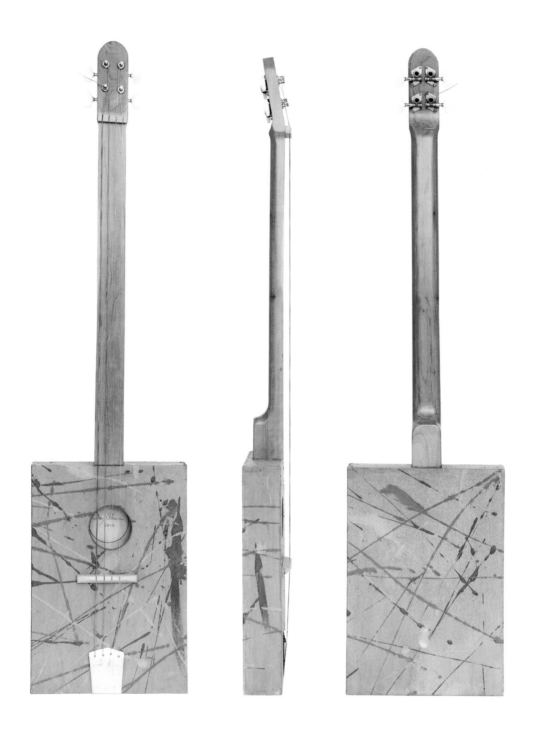

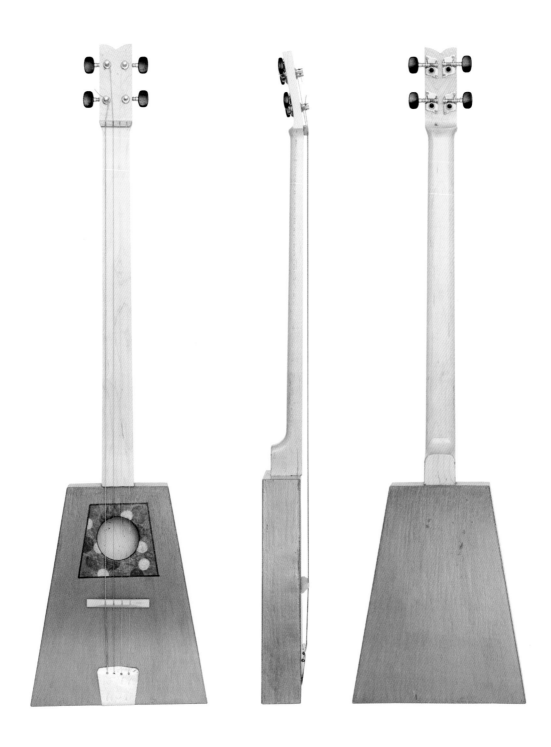

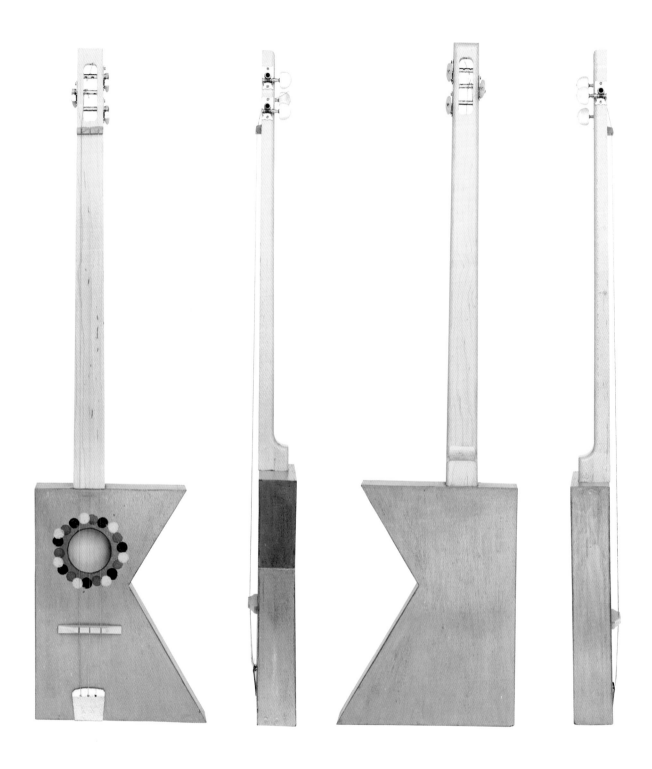

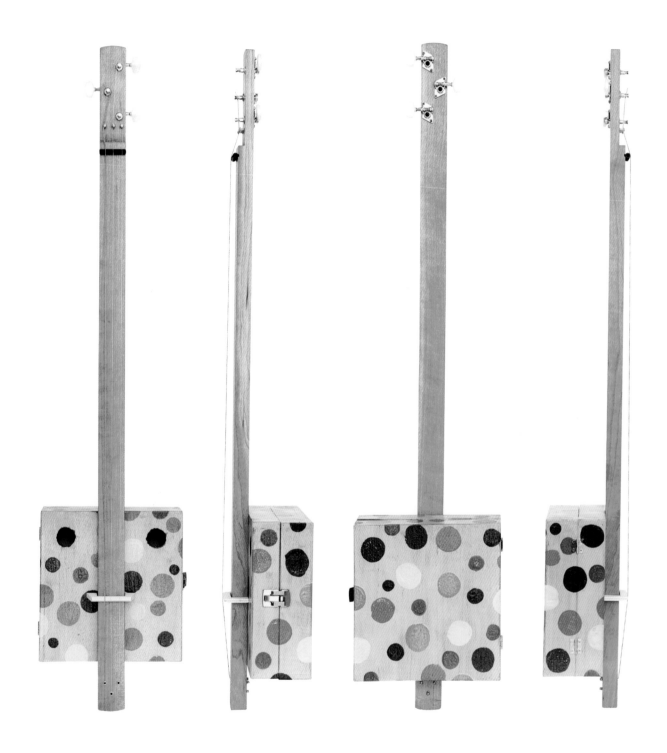

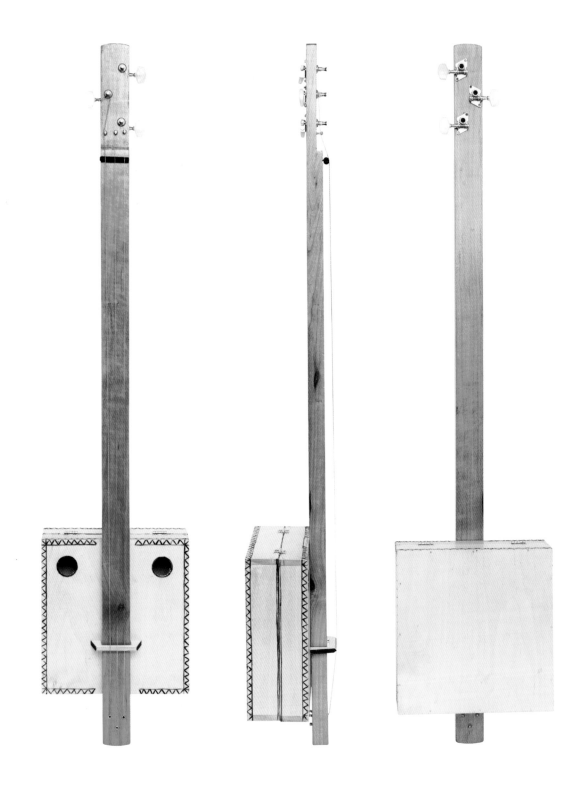

MAKERS' GALLERY

The world of guitar making is exciting and diverse. Take a look at these eight gifted guitar makers to get your own ideas!

Ron Lutz
EUREKA SPRINGS, ARKANSAS
studio62.biz

I'm a gallery owner, professional photographer, and woodworker. My handmade guitars and kalimbas are sold at my gallery, Studio 62 Eureka Springs. My interest in making instruments started 40 years ago with a banjo and several dulcimers. That interest was rekindled recently upon discovering the cigar box guitar community. Particularly useful are the skills gained from Doug Stowe's box making workshops at Eureka Springs School of the Arts. An admirer of the beauty of various woods, I enjoy repurposing wood from dead trees harvested from my land.

My advice is to always keep safety as a priority, plan each project, feel free to experiment, and most of all—have fun.

Two-string fretless bass guitar; the sound hole is a knot.

"Old Red" three-string fretless guitar, featuring dyed wood.

Three-string fretless guitar with maple neck.

Three-string fretless guitar; note the padauk position markers.

Ed Stilley
EUREKA SPRINGS, ARKANSAS

www.stillonthehill.com/edstilley and *www.stillonthehill.com/listen-stilley*

As a craftsman using only basic woodworking tools, a fertile imagination, and materials available to him from the forests of the Ozark Mountains, Ed Stilley made hundreds of guitars that he gave away to neighbors and children. His folk instruments are documented in a book by musician Kelly Mulhollan: *True Faith, True Light, the Devotional Art of Ed Stilley* from the University of Arkansas Press. Ed's work helped inspire me to cut loose and make without restraint.   —*Doug Stowe*

Color photographs shown with this profile by Kirk Lanier; black and white by Flip Putthoff; X-ray by Dr. Dennis Warren, used with permission of Kelly Mulhollan, author of *True Faith, True Light: The Devotional Art of Ed Stilley.*

Ed Stilley in 1987, still in his prime and making instruments at a furious pace. He has gathered a sampling of instruments still under construction in his workshop for newspaper reporter Flip Putthoff.

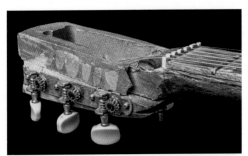

The butterfly guitar features dramatic proportions and an elaborate internal metallic skeleton consisting of a circular saw blade, door springs, aluminum pipe, and a steel truss rod.

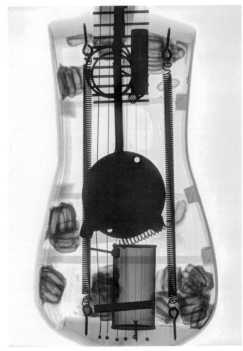

Ed's guitars are amazing folk art, not only for how they look, but for his unique way of addressing tonality. He used steel junk carefully fitted inside his guitar bodies to vibrate and provide resonance.

Zeke Leonard
SYRACUSE, NEW YORK
SCFOIW.blogspot.com

The oldest known human-made object that is not a tool is a 40,000-year-old flute made from a bird bone. It has holes drilled in it that make a scale that is recognizable even today. Making music, and especially making music together with other people, is inextricably woven into the fabric of our cultures, societies, and communities. Improvised instruments welcome makers of objects and music to come together, to make music, to listen to each other, and to enjoy each other's company. One of the things I find compelling about making musical instruments is the sheer delight that players and listeners feel when they play or listen to these instruments. They are really objects of joy. And they are not precious, but have about them an air of approachability. They ask to be examined, to be plucked, to be touched and held and played. Play yours in good health, and feel free to stop by and sit for a while and we'll play together!

Guitars embellished by the reverb community. From left to right: photo embellishment by Damian Vallelonga; ink work by Jaime Snyder; print by Jason Evans; woodburning based on a photo of the piano innards by Janie and Jonathan Mills; sign painting by Cayetano Valenzuela.

Tenor signed by Pete Seeger.

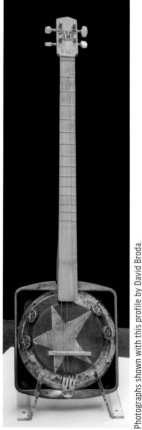

Starr Hill Bluesmaster Banjo.

Photographs shown with this profile by David Broda.

John McNair
SPARKS, NEVADA
reddogguitars.com

These guitars are made by hand, without power tools, because I enjoy learning how craftsmen did woodworking in early America and colonial times. I've been playing and working on guitars for almost 30 years, and enjoy building and selling them under the name Red Dog Guitars. I believe that life is short, so carefully crafting instruments is a way of sharing God's grace with others.

1937 Aviator, three-string cigar box guitar.

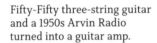

Fifty-Fifty three-string guitar and a 1950s Arvin Radio turned into a guitar amp.

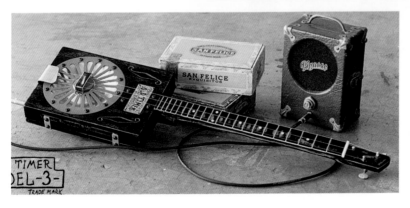

Three-string resonator cigar box guitar.

Ted Crocker
STUART, FLORIDA
handmademusicclubhouse.com

I formed the Handmade Music Clubhouse in 2009 for builders and players of all types of homemade instruments, with a spotlight on cigar box guitars. There is a wealth of information in the form of photos, forums, videos, blogs, and member pages. I've been active in the CBG movement since 2003, and have had some great experiences, including creating instruments for a movie and for performing artists. For some interesting stories and tips on building your own cigar box guitars, please visit the Clubhouse!

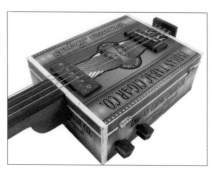

A rack full of stringed instruments.

Indian Tabac guitar.

Ginny for Ice Bob, featuring wood from the cotton gin at Hopson Plantation.

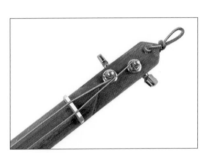

Gisbert drain reso, two-string with a cigar box and a floor drain reso cone.

Shane Speal
YORK, PENNSYLVANIA
www.ShaneSpeal.com

I'm an enthusiastic advocate of the cigar box guitar, and have been exploring this instrument through building and playing for more than two decades. A cigar box guitar is a primitive instrument made by the American poor folk. Don't overthink your first build. Put your creativity in the mindset of a person in the Depression Era who is too poor to order a guitar even from the Sears catalog. If you don't have all the right tools or parts, use whatever is available. Blues legends like Lightnin Hopkins and Furry Lewis didn't even have guitar strings when they made their first cigar box guitars, so they pulled wire out of their screen doors! And it worked! If you want to learn how to play your new instrument, check out the free lessons at my website.

Six-string broom stick CBG; a take on the classic "broom stick shoved in a cigar box" design.

Damned If I Do; an instrument that captures struggle, poverty, and the Blues within the artistic side of cigar box guitar building.

Tribute to Ed Stilley.

Richard Briggs
UPLAND, CALIFORNIA
www.cigarboxguitarsbyrich.com

I had a very stressful job as a sales rep, so I would make furniture after work to calm me down. After I retired, I couldn't afford to buy $400 of oak to make a piece of furniture; I looked around and found cigar box guitars. That Thanksgiving I showed my work to my family and they posted photos online. A local hospital contacted me and asked if I would make one and donate it for their silent auction fundraiser—one thing led to another and I'm having a ball. I meet the most interesting people! Through experience, I have settled on scale lengths of 24" (61cm) for my guitars and banjos and 17" (43cm) for my ukuleles. Necks are hand carved with a draw knife and the fretboards are usually yardsticks from hardware stores.

Krusty's three-string, a whimsical design made of leftovers.

Tambourine banjo, inspired by a request to make a banjo out of a tambourine.

Fishing uke, complete with a fishing lure as a bridge and a spoon in the fretboard.

Kevin Hamilton, HamBone Cigar Box Guitars
WYLIE, TEXAS

www.hambonecbg.com

I began building cigar box guitars in 2010 after I heard one and the sound haunted me afterward. What really started out as a hobby became a passion and continues to grow. Building these little cigar box guitars constantly challenges me. I enjoy the rudimentary quality of them, and I really like to see where I can take my next build. Whether it is building a custom order for someone or making whatever I think the box needs to become, it is a great creative outlet. The cigar box guitar has a great history behind it and we are continuing to write its story today.

The best tip for any new builder is just don't be afraid to try. All of the builders out there have made many mistakes and gained knowledge from those lessons. Reach out to other builders for advice; most are very willing to help. Remember, there are no rules in cigar box guitar building. Be creative and have fun.

American Beauty; it now belongs to Justin Johnson and has traveled to Paris and Amsterdam.

#5.

Hellhound resonator, with inlay by
Mr. Wizard's Inlay (Wayne McComic)
and a stainless-steel resonator cover
and tailpiece by Old Lowe.

Texas Star four-string; now owned by Jackie Don Loe, local Dallas/Fort Worth artist.

ILLUSTRATIONS

The illustrations provided here will help you in creating the different guitars shown through the book. To find the original page where each drawing is mentioned, flip to the listed page numbers with each illustration.

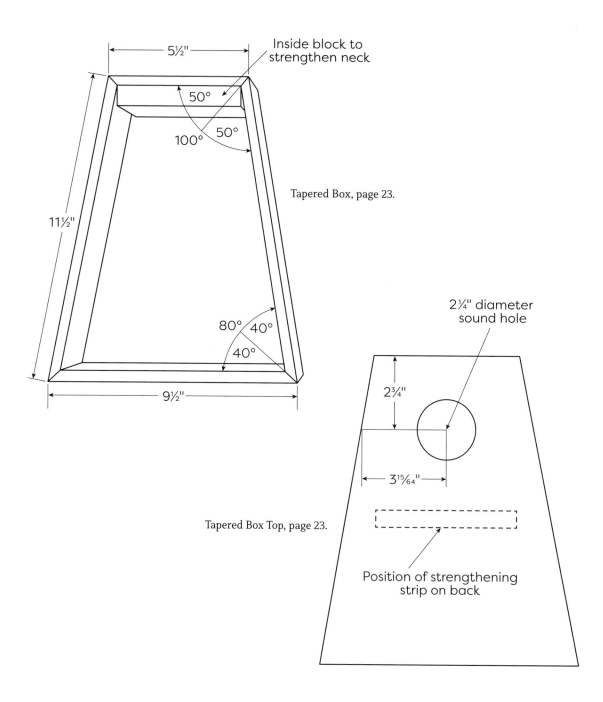

Inside block to strengthen neck

Tapered Box, page 23.

2¼" diameter sound hole

Position of strengthening strip on back

Tapered Box Top, page 23.

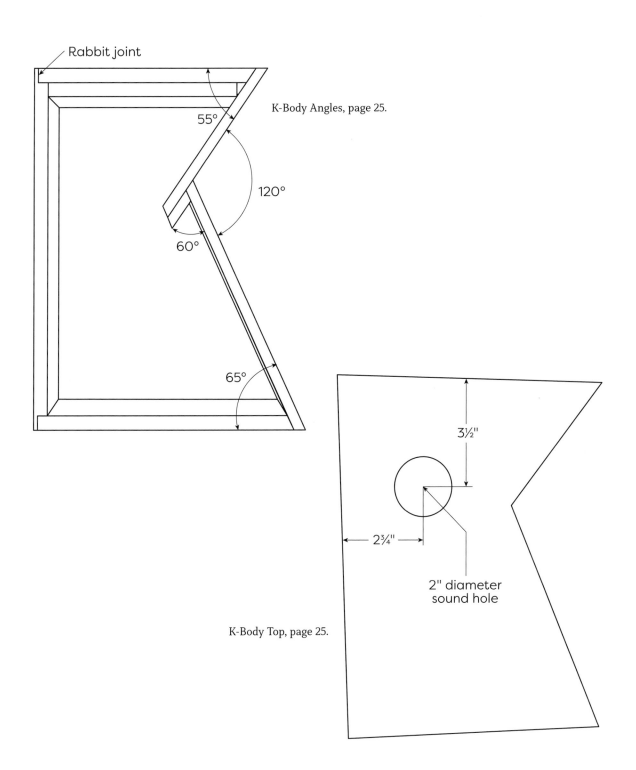

Rabbit joint

55°

120°

60°

65°

K-Body Angles, page 25.

3½"

2¾"

2" diameter
sound hole

K-Body Top, page 25.

K-Body Exploded Drawing, page 25.

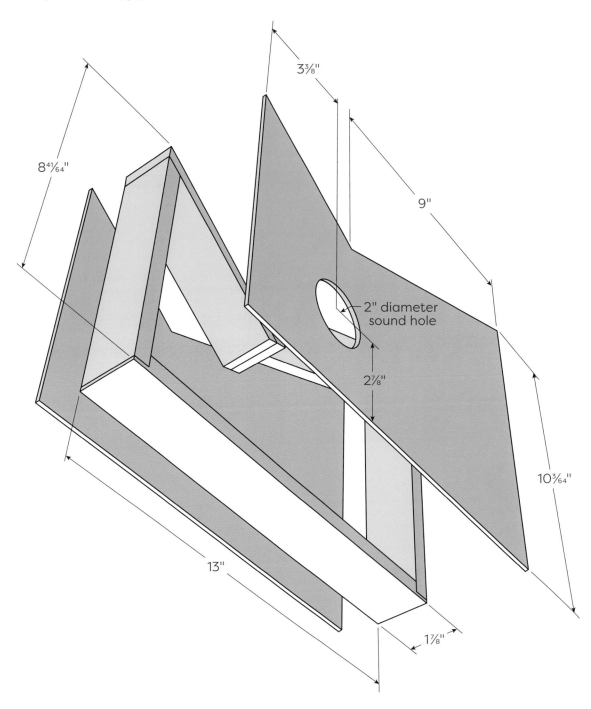

2" diameter sound hole

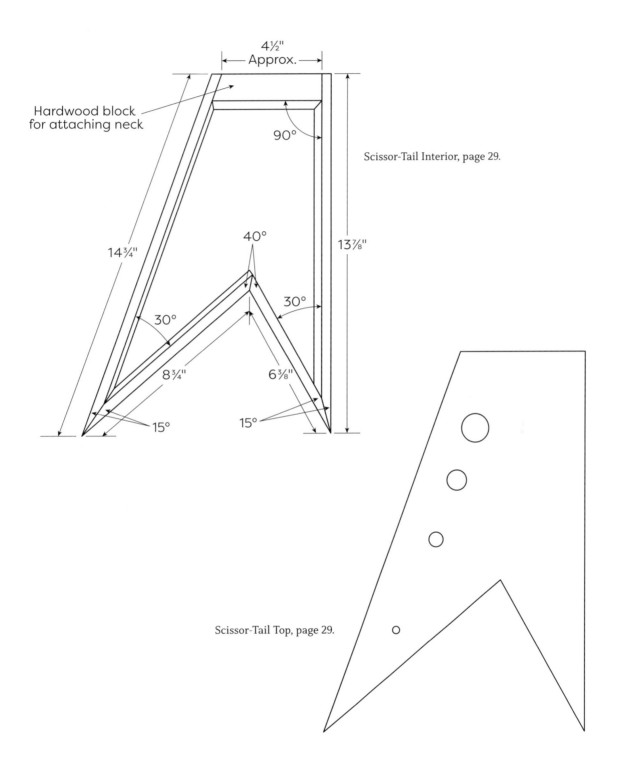

4½"
Approx.

Hardwood block
for attaching neck

90°

Scissor-Tail Interior, page 29.

14¾"

40°

30°

30°

13⅞"

8¾"

6⅜"

15°

15°

Scissor-Tail Top, page 29.

Keyed Miter Slide Jig Front, page 33.

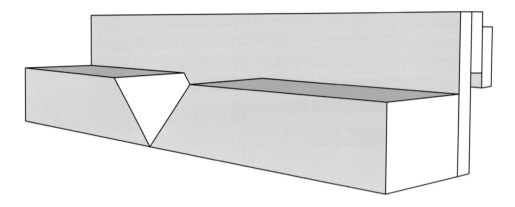

Keyed Miter Slide Jig Back, page 33.

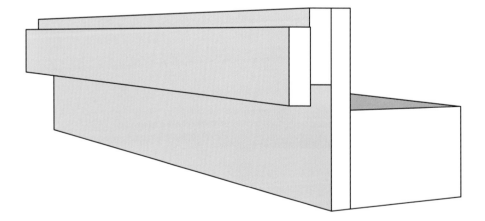

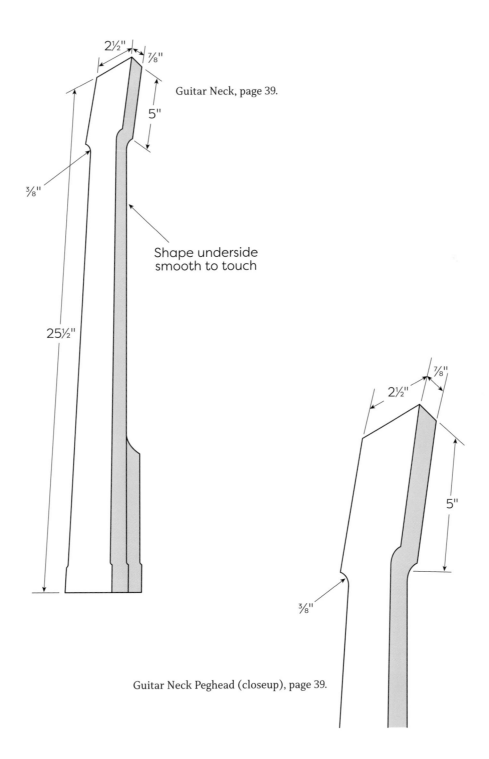

2½" ⁷⁄₈"

Guitar Neck, page 39.

5"

³⁄₈"

Shape underside
smooth to touch

25½"

⁷⁄₈"

2½"

5"

³⁄₈"

Guitar Neck Peghead (closeup), page 39.

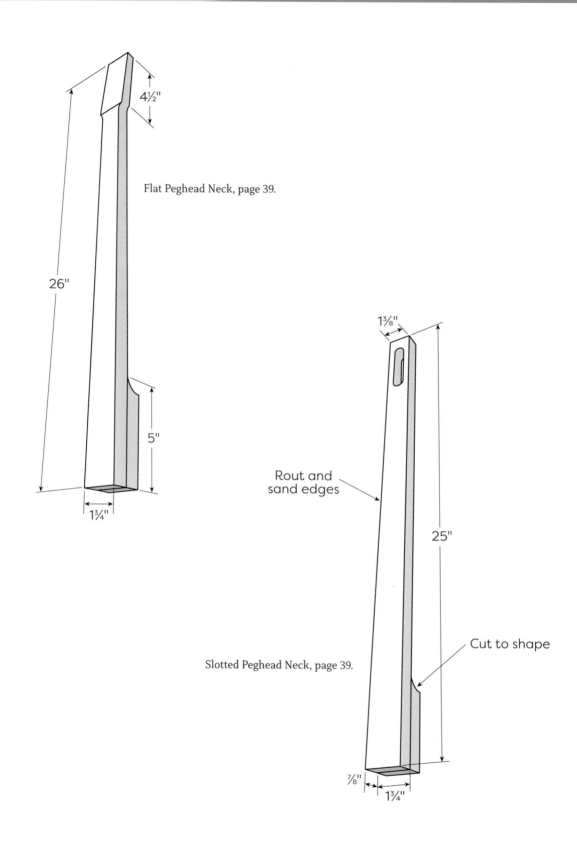

4½"

26"

Flat Peghead Neck, page 39.

5"

1¾"

1⅜"

Rout and
sand edges

25"

Cut to shape

Slotted Peghead Neck, page 39.

⅞"

1¾"

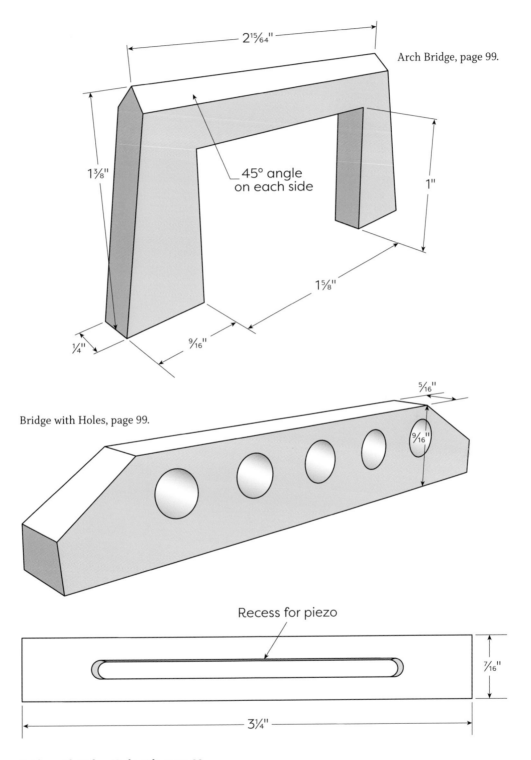

2$^{15}/_{64}$"

Arch Bridge, page 99.

1$^3/_8$"

45° angle
on each side

1"

1$^5/_8$"

$^1/_4$"

$^9/_{16}$"

Bridge with Holes, page 99.

$^5/_{16}$"

$^9/_{16}$"

Recess for piezo

$^7/_{16}$"

3$^1/_4$"

Bridge with Holes, Underside, page 99.

Guitar Electrifying Rig, page 105.
Courtesy of Ted Crocker.
For more wiring rigs, visit handmademusicclubhouse.com/photo/albums/wiring-diagrams-schematics

Piezo, Volume & Jack

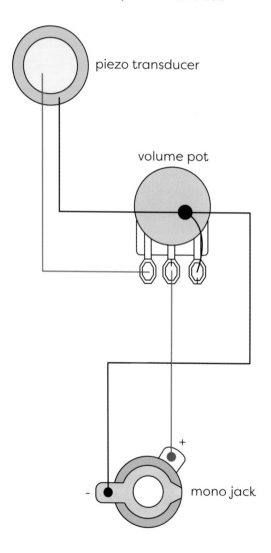

piezo transducer

volume pot

mono jack

+

-

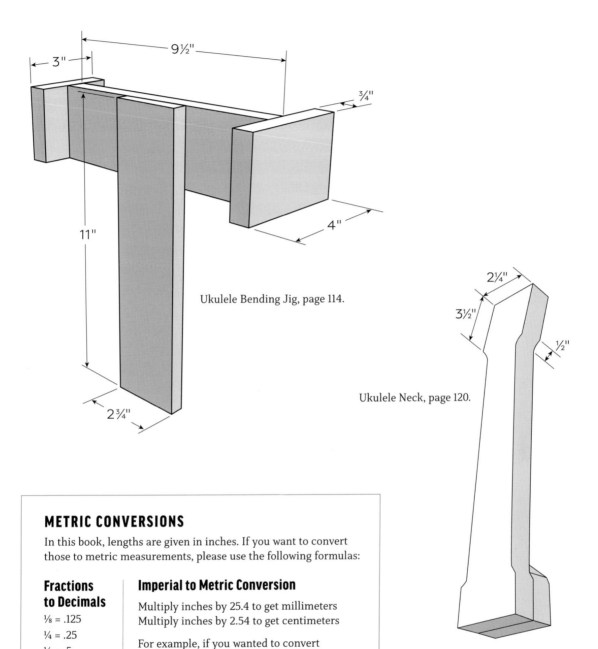

Ukulele Bending Jig, page 114.

Ukulele Neck, page 120.

METRIC CONVERSIONS

In this book, lengths are given in inches. If you want to convert those to metric measurements, please use the following formulas:

Fractions to Decimals

⅛ = .125
¼ = .25
½ = .5
⅝ = .625
¾ = .75

Imperial to Metric Conversion

Multiply inches by 25.4 to get millimeters
Multiply inches by 2.54 to get centimeters

For example, if you wanted to convert 1⅛ inches to millimeters:

• 1.125 in. x 25.4 mm = 28.575 mm

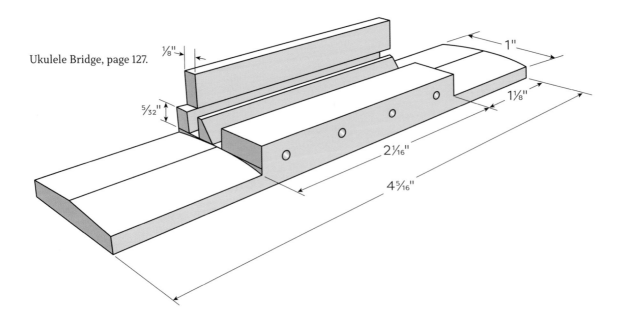

Ukulele Bridge, page 127.

1/8"

5/32"

1"

1 1/8"

2 1/16"

4 5/16"

Ukulele Bridge Jig, page 127.

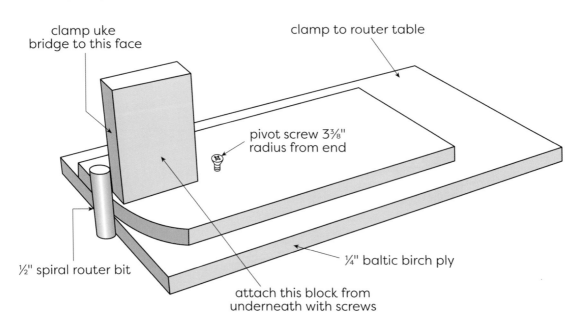

clamp uke bridge to this face

clamp to router table

pivot screw 3 3/8" radius from end

1/2" spiral router bit

1/4" baltic birch ply

attach this block from underneath with screws

INDEX

MORE GREAT BOOKS *from*
SPRING HOUSE PRESS

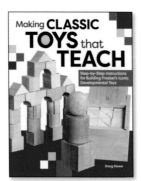

Making Classic Toys that Teach
978-1-940611-33-4
$24.95 | 144 Pages

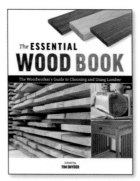

The Essential Wood Book
978-1-940611-37-2
$27.95 | 224 Pages

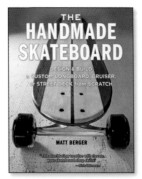

The Handmade Skateboard
978-1-940611-06-8
$24.95 | 160 Pages

Classic Wooden Toys
978-1-940611-34-1
$24.95 | 176 Pages

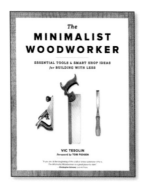

The Minimalist Woodworker
978-1-940611-35-8
$24.95 | 152 Pages

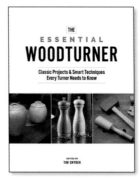

The Essential Woodturner
978-1-940611-47-1
$27.95 | 224 Pages

Make Your Own Knife Handles
978-1-940611-53-2
$24.95 | 168 Pages

The New Bandsaw Box Book
978-1-940611-32-7
$19.95 | 128 Pages

Make Your Own Cutting Boards
978-1-940611-45-7
$22.95 | 168 Pages

SPRING HOUSE PRESS

Look for these Spring House Press titles at your favorite bookstore, specialty retailer, or visit *www.springhousepress.com*.
For more information about Spring House Press, email us at *info@springhousepress.com*.